101

Cool Magic Tricks

Barb Whiter

Hinkler Books Pty Ltd

17-23 Redwood Drive

Dingley Victoria 3172

Australia

ISBN: 1 86515 713 9

Copyright © 2002 Hinkler Books Pty Ltd

First printed 2001

Written by Barb Whiter

Illustrated by Glen Singleton

Edited by Julie Haydon

Original page design by Chris Murphy

Final design and page layout by DiZign

Printed and bound in Australia

Contents

Introduction

So, you'd like to do magic tricks? Why?

If your answer is you'd like to perform in front of audiences at home, school, or even at community festivals, read on, and you'll get some great tips to create a captivating magic show.

If you just like the idea of learning some magic tricks to do in front of your family and close friends, that's fine too. Either way, this is the book for you, because there are so many tricks—101 in fact—contained in these pages. You will be able to keep everyone entertained for months!

Magic is found in the myths and legends of cultures throughout the world. You may have heard of Merlin the Magician, who trained King Arthur to become King of England more than 1,500 years ago. It was only Arthur who could pull the magic sword, Excalibur, from its rock prison (put there by Merlin), and so he became King.

Although most of us can't explain how a microchip powers our computer, or remember the principles of electricity once our science lesson is over, we accept what these and other marvels of technology can do for us. But who hasn't been surpsrised as a smiling magician makes a coin disappear, or reappear, seemingly at will? We love mysteries, and that's the appeal of magic.

Therefore, the first rule a magician must learn is—never, ever tell anyone how to do a trick. It doesn't matter if the person is your best friend.

DO NOT TELL HOW A TRICK IS DONE!

Getting Started

There are a few rules to remember when performing magic tricks:

1 Never tell anyone how a trick is done. I know we've said this before, but it's the first rule. DO NOT TELL!

2 Practice each trick until you can do it over and over without a mistake.

3 Keep your audience directly in front of you. Don't let people sit beside or behind you.

4 Don't repeat a trick in front of the same audience. It may be flattering to be asked to do so, but the members of your audience are only trying to see how the trick's done!

5 As a general rule, don't tell your audience what you are going to do. It's better to let anticipation and suspense build as you perform your trick. You can, however, talk to your audience. This will help distract them, so they will not see what you are really doing!

6 Use expressions and gestures to enhance your act. For example, you can frown to show you are concentrating hard; or stand still without speaking to gain your audience's attention; or you might like to use sweeping arm gestures when you are calling upon your "magical powers" or trying to distract your audience.

7 Make sure all your props are in perfect working order and look good—no scruffy wands or hats.

8 Once you have learned a trick and can perform it, you may choose to change it. This can be fun!

9 Practice and perfect the story you tell while performing each trick—it's what makes you different from another person who performs the same trick.

10 If you can, perform against a dark background under a good light.

Putting on a Magic Show

Begin by learning simple tricks that interest you, and require only a few props. You will find these tricks are the easiest to perform. As you become more confident, you can learn longer, more difficult tricks.

Then it will be time to plan your act!

Every well-planned act has a beginning, a middle, and an end. When planning your act, remember to place shorter tricks between longer ones. This will help to hold your audience's interest. Think about how long you want your show to be. When you are starting out, a good show is often a short show! Maybe you only want your show to last 10–15 minutes. That's still a lot of talking and a lot of tricks when you are new to magic!

Preparation

Besides the obvious, learning your tricks so you are really confident performing them—you need to have the props ready for every trick you perform. It is a good idea to cover a table with a cloth and put the props on top of the cloth until they are needed. Make sure your props look good!

Plan what you are going to wear. Dressing up like a magician, even if you don't rely on your costume for props, is a way of really making you look the part. You may want to wear something special for certain tricks, such as a jacket for the arm-stretching trick.

Also, if you have decided to weave a special story or line throughout the show, practice this as much as your tricks. You need to be confident with everything!

7

Performing

When you are in front of your audience, act confident. Look excited about the magic tricks you are performing. Take your bows and enjoy the applause—that's one of the reasons you are there.

Speak as clearly as you can. If you mumble, your audience won't be able to follow what you are saying, and may miss crucial pieces of information.

Always involve your audience by asking for volunteers, and don't worry if something goes wrong. Either repeat it, if appropriate, or begin the next trick.

Plan your show so your best trick is performed last, and you go out to loud applause!

Finally, have fun!

Quick Tricks and Simple Illusions

Begin your show with a couple of these quick
and simple illusions. They will have your audience
wanting more!

Trick 1
Long or short

★ **You need:** a pencil, a piece of paper, a ruler

This is an easy illusion to warm up your audience.

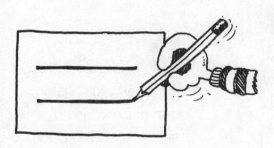

1 Draw two straight, parallel lines on the paper, making sure they are exactly the same length, say 2 in. (5 cm) each. Position them about 1 in. (2 cm) apart.

2 Then draw angles, as in the diagrams right, on the ends of each line. You know the lines are the same length, but it will be hard for your friends to see that, because an optical illusion makes one appear shorter than the other.

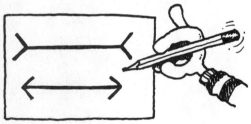

Step back my friends! This is a Magic Rabbit! ...it could be loaded!

Did you know?
Mandrake the Magician was a popular comic strip hero of the 1940s. He would often outwit his opponents by using his magical powers.

Trick 2
Magical number nine

★ **You need:** just a pair of hands—yours!

It's a good idea to create a story about the magical number nine for this one!

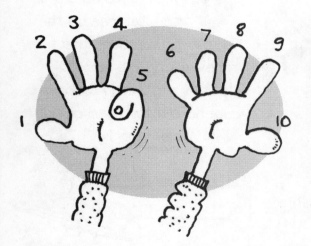

1 Did you know you can multiply by 9 easily, just using your fingers? Hold your hands up and, in your head, number your fingers from 1 to 10 starting with the little finger on your left hand.

2 Whichever number you wish to multiply by 9, bend down the finger with that number. How many fingers are left standing on either side of the bent finger? For example, to multiply 5 by 9, bend finger number 5 and count the fingers to the left and right of it. The answer is 4 on your left hand and 5 on your right hand, this is 45—right!

3 Try it with any multiple—up to 10 of course—it works every time!

CHAPTER 1

Trick 3
More nines

★ **You need:** a pencil, a piece of paper, a calculator (optional)

Keep up the illusion of nine being a magical number with this number trick.

9
18
27
36
45
54
63
72
81
+ 90
───
495

1 First, write down the number 9.
Then underneath, in a column, write down the multiples of 9. That is, 9 multiplied by 2, then by 3, and so on, up to 9 multiplied by 10. (You will know an easy way of doing this if you did the trick before this one!) Draw a line underneath these figures.

2 Add all the numbers together and you should get 495. Add these digits together, 4 + 9 + 5, and the answer is 18. By adding these digits together, 1 + 8, what do you get? Yes, 9!

3 Even if you add more multiples of 9 to the column you will always end up with the same answer—9. It's a spooky number, isn't it?

Trick 4
Mind-reading

★ **You need:** a pencil, a piece of paper, a calculator (optional)

Again, this mind-reading trick uses the "magical" number nine. Performed with the help of a friend, this trick will be a great addition to your show and really impress your audience!

1 Tell your friend to write down any three-digit number he likes, but the digits must decrease in value, such as 9, 7, and 2. He must not let you see what he's written.

2 Then tell your friend to write the same number backwards, underneath the first—that would be 2, 7, and 9.

3 Now tell him to subtract this number from the first and tell you only the final digit. In our example, this is 3.

4 Immediately tell him the remaining numbers are 6 and 9, because you subtract the 3 from the 9 to find the first digit—that is 6. The middle digit is always 9, no matter what three-digit number your friend chose! There's that sneaky 9 again!

Trick 5
More mind-reading

★ **You need:** a pencil, a piece of paper, a calculator

Tricks that involve mind-reading and numbers are always fascinating. Here's another easy and effective one to include in your show.

1 Ask a friend to write down a number. It can be any number she likes (it doesn't matter how many digits) provided the digits increase in value. She is not to show you the number until the end of the trick.

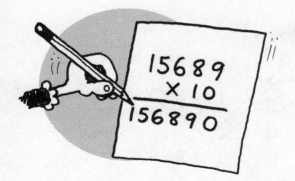

$$15689 \times 10$$
$$156890$$

2 Ask your friend to multiply the number she wrote down by 10. (Let's pretend your friend chose the number 15689.)

3 Ask your friend to subtract the first number from the second number.

$$156890 - 15689$$
$$141201$$

$$141201$$
$$+ 9$$
$$141210$$

4 Ask your friend to add 9 to the answer.

5 Have your friend cross out any number she likes except for a zero. She should tell you what the remaining digits are. In our example, the second 1 is crossed out, and the remaining numbers are 1, 4, 2, and 1.

141/210

6 Add these remaining digits in your head. They come to 8. Then subtract the total from 9 to find out what number was crossed out.

7 Tell your friend the number she crossed out was 1! Mind-reading wins again!

1
CHAPTER

Trick 6
Arrows abound

★ **You need:** a pencil, a sheet of paper, a glass (straight-sided), a jug of water, a table

This magic trick is a great one to do before a small audience.

1 Fold the sheet of paper in half and draw an arrow in the middle of one side. It doesn't matter which way the arrow faces.

2 Stand the folded sheet on a table with the arrow facing the audience. Place the empty glass in front of it. Now challenge a member of the audience face the arrow the other way without touching the paper or the glass.

3 Of course, he can't do it (unless unhappily he has seen the trick done before!), but you can by producing the jug of water (which until now has been out of sight) and filling the glass with water.

4 Hey presto! The arrow turns to face the opposite way!

Now...don't take your eyes off this cabbage for a second ...as its about to disappear!

My... whats that over there?

Did you know?
Magicians are often very theatrical performers, more so than actors! Magicians use grand gestures to distract audiences from what is really happening during a show!

1

CHAPTER

Trick 7
Magic paper rings

★ **You need:** a paper strip about 12 in. (30 cm)
by 1.5 in. (4 cm), glue, scissors

This quick little illusion will have your audience believing you
can do anything!

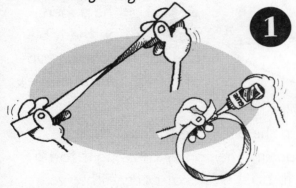

1 Hold the paper strip
and twist it once.

2 Then glue the
ends together.

3 Cut around the center of
the ring carefully. What's
the result? Two rings? No, it's one
big ring if you've cut correctly.

4 Now to take this a
little further—cut
around the centre again.
Do you think you'll get a really
big ring this time? No! This
time there are two rings!

Trick 8

Can you do it?

★ **You need:** a sheet of paper, an unopened can of food, a table

---

You should show this trick only once to any one audience.

1 Lay the paper flat on the table and put the can on top of it (right in the middle).

2 Challenge anyone in the audience to remove the paper without touching the can or allowing it to tip over. No one will be able to do it, unless of course they've seen the trick performed elsewhere! But you can!

3 Pick up the longer side of the paper and begin to roll it into a tube. As the paper tube reaches the can, keep rolling. Do not touch the can. The tube will move the can away from you. Keep on rolling the paper until the can has moved completely off the paper, and you can wave your rolled tube in a salute!

Trick 9
Something goes!

★ **You need:** a coin, a blunt pencil

Tell your audience you can make a coin disappear, but it seems you need more practice!

1 Stand with your left side toward your audience, if you are right-handed, or your right side towards them, if you are left-handed. Put the coin in the hand closest to the audience, and hold it up, explaining that it will disappear once you tap it sharply three times with your pencil.

2 Hold the end of the pencil with the fingers of your other hand and bring it up into the air until it is level with your ear.

ONE!

3 Bring the pencil down and tap the coin sharply with it while exclaiming a really loud "One".

4 Do this again, bringing the pencil up to exactly the same height and down again, tapping the coin, and saying "Two".

THREE!

5 Without missing a beat, bring the pencil up one more time. This time, slide it easily and quickly behind your ear. Bring your empty hand down, saying "Three", and look really surprised to discover the pencil has vanished.

6 Turn away from the audience, without showing the pencil if possible, and mutter something about having to practice the trick some more.

7 Remember—to succeed with this trick, you need to keep the same "beat" going when counting. Don't pause between any of the taps of the coin, especially not before the third tap!

Hey... I'm not a happy Pharoah.../ What happened to the Vanishing Pyramid Trick and turning a camel into a palm tree?

Did you know?

The first record of performing magicians is in the Westcar Papyrus in the State Museum of Berlin, Germany. It contains documented proof that magicians performed for the Pharaohs of Ancient Egypt about 4500 years ago.

CHAPTER 1

Trick 10

The coin really disappears this time...

★ **You need:** a coin, a pencil, a table

This trick works beautifully after the previous one, but can be a stand-alone trick if you prefer.

1 Begin by sitting at a table with your side to the audience. If your dominant hand (that is the hand you do most things with) is your right hand, sit with your left hand toward the audience, and vice versa, if you are left-handed.

2 Repeat trick 9, but do it sitting down. When you count "Three", act surprised the pencil has vanished, and look questioningly at the audience. At first, they'll be surprised too, but then you should let them see the pencil stuck behind your ear. They'll begin laughing. You should laugh too.

THREE!

3 Reach up with your dominant hand to remove the pencil. Now here's the clever part, while you are removing the pencil with one hand (and hopefully the whole audience is watching you do that), the hand holding the coin quickly tips it into your lap.

4 As the coin leaves your hand, close your hand into a fist (you want the audience to think you are still holding the coin).

5 Say something like: "Well I tricked you there, but now let me really make the coin disappear". Lift the pencil, and tap your closed fist with it. Then open your hand to show the coin is gone!

Trick 11
It's always 1089

★ **You need:** two pieces of paper, an envelope,
a pencil, a table, a calculator (optional)

With this quick trick, you'll convince your audience you have
special power!

1 Place your props on
the table and stand in
front of your audience.
Talk about the power of the
mind, telepathy and reading
thoughts. Say something like:
"There is always someone in my
audience whose mind is open
to me". Then, stop and say
there is someone in the audience whose thoughts you are
picking up right now. Point to a person in the audience.

2 Pretend to be thinking
hard, and ask the
"telepathic" person to
concentrate on transmitting his
thoughts to you. Say you think a
number is coming through to you.
Quickly write down 1089 on a
piece of paper, place it in the
envelope, and seal it.

3 Hand the other piece of paper and the pencil to the "telepathic" person, and ask him to write down any three figure number where all the digits are different (in our example, we've used the number 341.) Now ask him to reverse the number, and subtract the smaller from the larger one. Ask him to write down a three-digit answer even if the first digit is zero.

4 Have him reverse this last number, and add the last two numbers together. Ask him to read his answer out loud to the rest of the audience. Now ask him to open the envelope, and read the number you wrote down. Both numbers will be 1089.

Boy.... That's really spooky! How does she do it?

5 The number is always 1089, so you only want to do this trick once in front of the same audience!

1
CHAPTER

Trick 12
Pocket puzzler

> ★ **You need:** a deck of cards, a calculator,
> a piece of paper, a pencil

Using your magical powers, you are able to name the card hidden in an assistant's pocket.

1 Ask a volunteer to come forward and write down any four-digit number on a piece of paper, without letting you see any of the numbers. The only condition is the four numbers must be different. (In our example, we'll use the number 7539.)

2 Ask him to add the four numbers together, and write down the total. Now give him the calculator, and ask him to subtract the total from the original number.

3 Hand the volunteer a deck of cards, and ask him to secretly remove four cards which have the same numbers as the four digits (an ace = 1 and a king = 0). Each card must be a different suit.

4 Ask your volunteer to put one card (which isn't a king) in his pocket, or out-of-sight, and hand you the other three cards. In our example, the volunteer puts the five of clubs in his pocket.

5 Now mentally add the values of the three cards. If the answer has more than one digit, add those digits until there is only one digit. (For example, 13 becomes 1 + 3 = 4).

6 Mentally subtract this number from 9, and the value of the card in your volunteer's pocket will appear, as if by magic! It's a five, and because you are holding cards which are hearts, spades, and diamonds, the card must be the five of clubs!

7 The only exception to this clever little trick is when you mentally subtract the value of the cards from 9 and the answer is 0, the missing card isn't a king, it's a 9.

Clever Card Tricks

Many young magicians include card tricks in their magic shows. This is a good idea. Almost every household has a deck of cards lying around, so no extra money needs to be spent on props.
There are many simple card tricks you can learn that look great when performed!

Trick 13
Who's lying?

★ **You need:** a deck of cards, a table

Card tricks are a magician's staple. Everyone expects you to be able to flip, shuffle, twist and read cards telepathically, so let's get to it!

1 Before your audience arrives, shuffle the deck of cards. Make sure you know which card is on the bottom.

2 Once your audience is seated, fan out the deck of cards on the table in front of you, and ask a volunteer to choose one card. She is not to show or tell you what it is.

3 While the volunteer looks at the card, you should close the fan of cards, straighten the deck, and place it on the table, face-down. Ask the volunteer to cut the deck into two equal piles.

4 Now ask your volunteer to put her card on the pile she cut from the top of the deck, then place the other half of the deck on top of this. This means the card you memorized from the bottom of the deck is on top of the selected card.

5 Now is the time for some good magician talk. Explain to the audience the deck of cards is special, it can detect lies!

6 Explain to your volunteer that you are going to turn each card over, and ask her if this is the card she selected. She is to say "No" every time, even when you turn over her selected card. The deck of cards will "tell" you when she is lying. Obviously, you are looking for the card you memorized. The card after it will be the selected card.

My magic pack of cards tells me you might be telling fibs!

7 When you turn over the selected card and your volunteer says "No", yell "Liar"! and watch her reaction!

CHAPTER 2

Trick 14
Picture perfect

★ **You need:** An old deck of cards, a table, a blindfold, a pin

Amaze your audience with this simple trick. You'll find all the picture cards in the deck while blindfolded!

1 Prepare the cards before your show. Using a pin, make a tiny hole near the top of each picture card, but not through any of the colors on the card. All the picture cards will have a small mark that you will be able to feel with your eyes closed.

2 Once your audience arrives, shuffle the cards and lay them facedown on the table. Tell your audience that your magic powers allow you to pick out all picture cards in the deck, while blindfolded.

3 Ask for a volunteer from the audience to cover your eyes with the blindfold.

4 Now take one card after another from the deck, and feel it with your fingertips for a few seconds. When you feel the small hole, you will know it is a picture card, so set it aside. Your audience will not be able to work out how you do it!

Trick 15
Balancing act

★ **You need:** one playing card, a plastic cup (not glass!)

Simple tricks are good tricks! Practice this one, and you'll look like a great magician, and don't forget your talk. This is the story you tell while performing magic. It's exclusively yours, even if the tricks are old!

1 Hold the card with the face (that is the suit and number) toward the audience. If you are right-handed, hold it in your left hand, and if you are left-handed, hold it in your right hand. Your thumb should be on one side of the card, and the middle, ring, and little fingers on the other. Your forefinger or index finger rests behind the card.

2 With your other hand, and while talking constantly to your audience about your magical powers, gently place the cup on top of the card. Place it so the cup is three-quarters behind the card, and move your index finger up to the bottom of the cup to hold it steady.

3 From the front it looks as though the cup is just sitting there, perfectly balanced on the card!

2
CHAPTER

Trick 16
The mysterious missing card

★ **You need:** a deck of cards (with a piece of double-sided tape on the back of the top card), a table

It doesn't matter which card your volunteer chooses from the pack, you can make it disappear immediately with this trick.

DOUBLE SIDED TAPE

1 Stand toward your audience with the deck of cards in your hand. Fan out the cards between both hands, so the card faces are facing your audience. (This also hides the piece of tape on the back of the top card, which you've already put in place!)

2 Select one person from the audience to study the cards. Ask her to take a card from the deck. Have her show her card to the audience.

3 Once she has chosen a card, close the fan, and hold the deck upright, still showing the card face to the audience. If you are left-handed, hold the deck in your right hand, and if you are right-handed, hold the deck in your left hand.

4 While you were doing this, your volunteer should have shown everyone else the card she chose. Now, take it back with your free hand, keeping the face away from you, and place it with a flourish back on the deck on top of the double-sided tape! Make sure the card fits exactly on top of the other so it looks like there is only one card.

5 Now, place the deck face-down on the table, and cut the cards. Explain to your audience that you are going to make the chosen card disappear. Say "Sim Sala Bim", wave your hands, or snap your fingers before turning over the cards and spreading them out on the table. Ask your volunteer to find the card she chose earlier. Of course, she cannot. The card has disappeared! Take a bow!

> SIM SALA BIM all right! It must be some kind of trick!

6 If you prefer, you can keep the cards in your hands, cut them, and count them out on to the table. Voilà, there are only 51, and the chosen card has "vanished".

Trick 17
The chosen card

> ★ **You need:** a deck of cards, a table

This trick requires some preparation, but when it's done properly, it's a real winner!

1 Separate the cards by making a pile of red cards and a pile of black cards. Put one pile on top of the other, so you have a deck of cards separated into two colored halves. Now, it's time to take it before your audience!

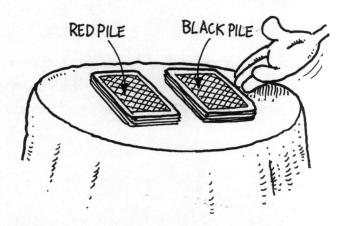

RED PILE   BLACK PILE

2 Pick up the cards and hold the deck face-down in your left hand, if you are right-handed, and in your right hand, if you are left-handed. With your other hand, begin to flick the cards with your thumb at the end nearest you. You are the only one who can see the faces of the cards. Flick from the bottom of the deck.

You don't have to actually see the numbers and suits, you want to see when the colors change. While you are doing this, explain to the audience that you are going to cut the deck into two equal piles.

3 Once the color changes, stop, and cut the deck. Only you know that the deck is in equal piles of different colored cards. Your audience thinks you have just cut the cards into two roughly equal piles, especially when you say: "I think the piles look the same."

4 Ask for a volunteer.

5 Take one pile and spread the cards face-down in your hands, and ask the volunteer to take a card, and memorize it. He can even show the card to the rest of the audience.

6 While he is doing that, put down those cards and pick up the other pile. Spread this one out in the same way, and tell your volunteer to place the selected card into this half of the deck.

7 Put the cards together again to make one deck, and ask your volunteer if he would like to cut the deck. He can do this as many times as he likes. It doesn't matter how many times the cards are cut. You will see clusters of the same colored cards together. When you see one card of the other color in amongst these clusters, you will know this is the chosen card.

8 However, do not let your volunteer shuffle the cards— if he does, you will not be able to find the chosen card! Also, it is possible that the chosen card will end up on the top or the bottom of the pack. If you cannot see a single card of a different color in a cluster in the deck, then check the top or bottom card. If you find a card of a different color, it is the chosen card.

Trick 18

Keep trying!

★ **You need:** a deck of cards, a table

This trick relies on good talking skills. Keep your audience interested and intrigued, even though you seem to be having trouble with the trick work. It also relies on good mathematics skills! Read on...

1 To begin, deal three columns of seven cards. Deal them on to the table, from left to right (this is very important) and face-up. Make sure you can see the number and suit of each card. Put the rest of the cards to one side – you won't need them for this trick.

2 Ask a volunteer to mentally choose a card, but not to name or touch the card. Then pretend to study the cards, as though trying to magically sense which one has been selected.

3 Tell your volunteer you seem to be having trouble magically sensing the card. Ask her to tell you which column it is in.

4 When she tells you which column, pick up each of the three columns of cards, keeping them face-up. You must pick up the columns so that the column she has chosen is in between the other two.

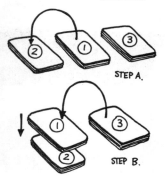

STEP A.

STEP B.

5 Deal three columns of seven cards again, exactly as before. Frown and pretend to be searching for the right card. You still can't find it!

6 Ask your volunteer again which column the card is in. Then repeat Step 4.

7 Keep talking to your audience while you deal three columns of cards and repeat Step 4 twice more. You need to deal the cards a total of four times for this trick to work.

8 By now you should be acting as though you are very annoyed! Tell your audience that you will try to pick the card one last time.

9 Begin dealing the cards as before – but this time, as you are dealing, count to the eleventh card in your head. Then stop suddenly, smile with relief, and hold up the card, announcing that "This" is the selected card!

10 This trick depends on mathematics, so you need to follow the directions exactly. It will work every time, but it's a good idea to practice it on your own before you do it in front of an audience.

Trick 19
The talking cards

★ **You need:** a deck of cards with no jokers, a table

You can find any card in a deck by listening to your "talking" cards...

1 Explain to your audience that you have special powers which enable you to hear "talking" cards—even though they won't be able to hear anything!

2 Ask a volunteer to deal out the cards face-up on the table. He must deal them out in a single row until you say "Stop". You should mentally count the number of cards being dealt, taking note of the seventh card. When your volunteer reaches 26, tell him to stop and say something like: "That should be enough cards to choose from".

3 Now tell the audience you'll select a card at random from those on the table, pretend to consider the cards. Then point to the seventh card. Ask your volunteer to tell the audience the name of the selected card. Explain to your audience that you will be able to find the selected card again with the help of your "talking" cards.

4 Pick up the cards, ensuring the seventh card stays in the seventh position. Put the cards face-down on the table in a pile, and put the rest of the deck on top.

5 Slowly deal out the cards, so they are face-up in a column. Tell the audience the cards are "talking" to you. Note the number of the first card. Continue to deal and silently count from that number until you reach 10. For example, if the first card is a 4, the next card becomes 5, then 6, 7, 8, 9, and 10, no matter what the numbers on the cards actually are.

6 Once you reach number 10, start another column—all the while pretending the cards are "talking" to you. If the first card you turn over in a column is a 10 or a face-card, such as a king or queen, it counts as 10, and so you must begin the next column. Aces count as 1.

7 Make three columns and then stop. Stare at the cards, and while the audience thinks you are "listening" to the cards, you should be adding up the first cards on the table

from each column, perhaps a 10, 3, and 2, which would make 15. This number is the key to finding the selected card! Remember to count the face cards as 10 and aces as 1.

8 Now, tell the audience the cards have told you the location of the selected card. Tell the volunteer to deal the same number of cards as your total—in our example, that is 15. The fifteenth card will be your selected card! The volunteer and audience will be amazed!

9 Try this trick a few times on your own or for your parents, and see how easy it is!

Trick 20
Choices

★ **You need:** a deck of cards, a table

In this trick, you ask a volunteer to deal a card seemingly at random—but, in fact, you already know the card's identity!

1 Before your show, memorize the tenth card from the top of a deck of cards, face up or face down.

2 Begin the trick by giving a volunteer the pack of cards. Ask her to think of a number between 10 and 20. Then, ask her to deal that number of cards face-down into a pile on the table. The rest of the deck can be put aside.

3 Now your volunteer needs to add together the two digits that make up the number she selected. If she selected the number 14, for example, she would add 1 and 4 to get 5. She then deals that number of cards, 5, from the pile and looks at the fifth card without telling anyone what it is. This card will be the card you memorized before the trick, the tenth card.

4 Pretend to read the volunteer's mind. Maybe you'd like to create more drama by drawing the card on a piece of paper, or you could ask the volunteer to return the card to the deck and shuffle the cards. She hands the deck to you and you "select" the card by "reading her fingerprints!"

5 However you do it, you'll be right every time!

Trick 21
ESP card

★ **You need:** a deck of cards, an envelope, a card from another deck of cards

In this trick, you hold a sealed envelope up before your audience and tell them there is a card inside. Select a card—seemingly at random—and it matches the card inside the sealed envelope!

1 Before your audience arrives, find the card (we'll call it card 1) in the full deck which matches the single card (card 2) you have taken from another deck. Place card 1 tenth from the top in the deck.

2 Seal card 2 in the envelope.

3 Introduce this trick by telling your audience there is a card in the sealed envelope. Ask a volunteer to hold the sealed envelope.

4 Hand the full deck to another volunteer and ask him to select a card. The final card dealt will be card 1 which, of course, matches the card in the envelope.

5 Ask the first volunteer to open the envelope and everyone will be sure you have special powers.

Trick 22
Topsy turvy

★ **You need:** a deck of cards, a table, a wand (optional)

Make a magician out of your volunteer with this trick. Your volunteer will pick a card, place it back in the deck, wave a magic wand—and presto!—the card will have magically turned over in the deck!

1 Before the audience arrives, turn over the bottom card, so the deck looks the same on both ends.

2 Select a volunteer. Spread the cards out face-down on the table—taking care not to show the reversed card on the bottom of the deck. Ask your volunteer to select a card, and show it to the audience, but not to you.

3 As the volunteer is showing the card to the audience, close the deck in the palm of one hand, and secretly turn it over so the reversed bottom card is now on top of the deck. You need to practice this movement to make it so smooth that no one will notice it.

4 Ask your volunteer to place the card face-down anywhere she likes in the deck. She placed the selected card backwards in the deck.

5 Now tell the volunteer she is going to perform the magic trick with the help of your magic wand (if you have one), or by speaking some magic words that you tell her. Turn over the hand holding the deck, so it is now palm down, and put the deck of cards flat on the table. The deck is right-side up again with the reversed card on the bottom of the deck. The selected card is also reversed.

6 Once your volunteer has woven her magic spell over the cards, you can pick up the deck, and spread the cards in a fan on the table, or move them from hand-to-hand until you come to the selected card, which of course will be reversed face-up within

the deck. Show the audience the card. Congratulate your new assistant, and enjoy the applause the two of you get!

Did you know?

In England, in the early 1700s, magic was considered respectable entertainment. Magicians performed in private homes, at booths at village fairs, and in theaters.

2
CHAPTER

Trick 23
Create an image

★ **You need:** a deck of cards in its box,
a small mirror, glue, a table

This trick relies on a good set-up!

1 Before your audience arrives, glue a small make-up mirror to the back of the card box. This may need to dry overnight. Keep the deck of cards in the box, with the flap closed.

2 To begin your performance, hold the box of cards in one hand with the mirror facing towards you. Remove the deck of cards with the other hand, and spread the cards on the table face-down. Continue to hold the box.

3 Ask someone in the audience to choose a card, look at it, memorize it, and then hand it to you. The card face must be turned away from you.

4 Take the card, making sure the face is still turned toward the audience and your volunteer, and say something like: "I need the help of the magic box to see the suit and number of the card." Then move the card behind the box so it is possible for you to glimpse the card in the mirror.

5 Keep the talk going by asking your volunteer to concentrate on the card he chose, and send a mental image of it to you. Place the box on the table (once you know what the card is!), so the mirror can't be seen, and put the card on top of the box so it will release its magic powers. Then proudly tell the audience what card the volunteer chose!

6 Don't do this trick more than once before the same audience, because it is too easy for someone to ask why you are holding the box. Someone may even see the mirror!

Trick 24
Arise card

★ **You need:** a deck of cards

Make any card you name rise out of the deck.

1 Ask a volunteer to shuffle the deck of cards.

2 When the deck is handed back to you, straighten it, taking note of which card is face-down on top. Perhaps it is the ten of diamonds.

TAKE A PEEK OF THE TOP CARD

3 Hold the deck vertically in one hand (left, if you are right-handed, and right if you are left-handed), so the cards are facing the audience.

PUSH ON AND UPWARDS WITH THIS FINGER

4 Place your other hand behind the deck and rest your forefinger, or index finger on top of the deck. Now extend your little finger (or ring finger if it is easier) until it touches the back of the top card (the ten of diamonds).

5 Now all you need to do is name the card, and ask it to rise for you! "Ten of diamonds...arise now from your slumber!" While you are saying this, push upwards on the top card with your little or ring finger, do it slowly, making sure your forefinger or index finger is rising as you speak. From where the audience is sitting, it will look as if your forefinger or index finger is encouraging the rising card to rise, and it will also look as if the card is coming from the middle of the deck. Easy but effective!

2
CHAPTER

Trick 25
Do drop in

★ **You need:** a deck of cards, a hat

This is another simple trick that is easy to set up and perform. It's a good one to do at the beginning of a magic show.

1 Ask for a volunteer to act as your assistant. Give your new assistant half the deck of cards.

2 Place the hat upside down on the floor in front of you. Take a card, and hold it a little over 3-4 feet (1 meter) above the center of the hat, and tell your audience you can get more cards into the hat than your assistant.

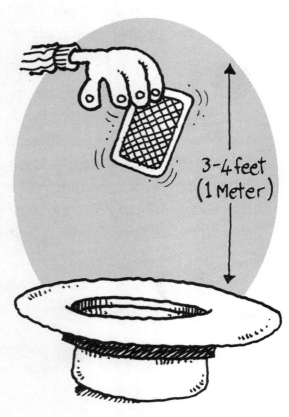

3-4 feet
(1 Meter)

3 Take a card and hold it by one end. You are just demonstrating how to drop the cards into the hat. If you let yours go, it probably won't go in the hat, and everyone will laugh! That's OK, in fact, that's really good!

4 Now get your assistant to drop her cards into the hat one at a time. The majority of the cards will miss the hat, and fall onto the floor. When your assistant has no cards left, count the cards that made it into the hat. Pick up the cards which didn't get into the hat, and make a big noise about how poorly your assistant did!

5 Now you get to show off! Hold your cards flat between your fingers and thumb facing the floor. As you drop each card, the cards will fall straight down (not float and spin as before). If you are standing directly over the hat, nine out of ten cards will go in the hat!

Trick 26
The magic wand

★ **You need:** a deck of cards, a table

Use your volunteer's hand as a magic wand! Everyone will be amazed!

1 Spread out the deck of cards, facedown in your hand, and have a volunteer pick a card. Then ask your volunteer to place their card facedown on the table, so you don't see it.

2 While your volunteer is looking at her card, close the deck of cards. Secretly take a look at the card on the bottom of the deck.

3 Now place the deck on top of your volunteer's card. Have your volunteer cut the deck once.

4 Pick up the deck and spread out all the cards, face-up, on the table. Look for your volunteer's card. It is immediately above the card you saw on the bottom of the deck.

5 Tell your volunteer you are going temporarily turn her hand into a magic wand, by sprinkling magic dust on to it. Reach into your pocket, and bring out some imaginary magic dust. Sprinkle it over her hand, saying "Sim Sala Bim!"

> SIM SALA BIM!
> Now that's a magic hand if I've ever seen one!

6 Take your volunteer's hand, and guide it over the cards. When you go over the card your volunteer chose, vibrate her hand, saying, "The magic wand shows this is the card!"

> WOW! Feel that VIBRATION? That's got to be the card!

7 Before your volunteer returns to the audience, snap your fingers, and say her hand is returned to normal.

Trick 27
What's gone?

★ **You need:** a deck of cards, a table, a chair

You'll need to concentrate while performing this trick, but do it well, and you'll earn yourself a reputation as a good magician.

1 First, remove the 10s, Jacks, Queens, and Kings from your deck of cards. Then hand nine cards, ace through nine, in any suit to one person in the audience.

2 Ask your new assistant to shuffle the cards. While they are shuffling, you should take a seat with your back to the table.

3 Tell your assistant to deal the cards into three rows with three cards in each.

4 Now ask your assistant to remove one card, show it to the audience, and put the card in her pocket.

5 Have the assistant (who is really doing all the work!) add up the cards in the columns, ignoring the space for the removed card.

6 Now, have your assistant add up the digits in the answer, in our example, that would be $1 + 0 + 1 + 5 + 1 + 3 = 11$. Your assistant tells you the total, which in this case is 11. Without pausing, or turning around, press your fingers to your head and say: "You removed the 7".

7 Get the answer by subtracting the answer your assistant gave from 9, or a multiple of 9. For instance, we know that 11 cannot be subtracted from 9, so for any number greater than 8, subtract it from 18. ($18 - 11 = 7$) You're right! If your assistant's answer is greater than or equal to 18, subtract it from 27.

CHAPTER 2

Trick 28
Card telepathy

★ **You need:** a deck of cards, a table

In this simple, but effective trick, you will find the card a volunteer chose, by counting the cards off the bottom of the deck. This trick relies on your counting skills. The better you are at fanning, the easier it will be to fool your audience, so practice fanning the cards out in your hands!

1 First, ask for a volunteer to shuffle the deck of cards and hand them back to you.

2 Now here is the secret— count the bottom nine cards in the deck, but don't remove them from the rest of the deck. Don't let your audience see you do this!

Keep the 9 CARDS pushed down slightly

3 Here's where you'll need to practice. Fan out the cards in your hands, facedown. Be sure to push the other cards in the deck slightly ahead of your counted cards as you fan the deck out.

59

4 Ask your volunteer to pick a card, and memorize it before giving it back to you. Without looking at the card, slip it back into the deck, right on top of the counted cards.

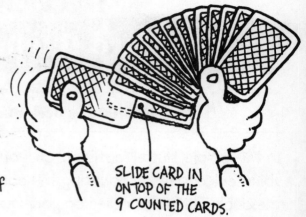

SLIDE CARD IN ON TOP OF THE 9 COUNTED CARDS.

5 Now close the deck of cards. Do not shuffle the cards any further, or your trick won't work.

6 Tell your audience you will use telepathy to learn which card your volunteer chose. Then slowly count the cards off the bottom of the deck, onto the table. When you come to the 10th card, stop, and hold it up. This is your volunteer's card!

Trick 29

It's time

★ **You need:** a deck of cards, a table, a watch

When you begin this trick, you might mention *Alice in Wonderland*'s White Rabbit, who was always looking at his watch and saying, "I'm late, I'm late, for a very important date." Your watch is a very important part of this trick.

1 Ask a volunteer from your audience to choose four cards from the deck.

2 The volunteer must decide which of the four cards is her favorite. While she decides this, divide the rest of the cards into two equal piles.

3 Ask your volunteer to place her favorite card on one of the piles. Now ask her to place the other three cards on top of the other pile. Do not look at the cards.

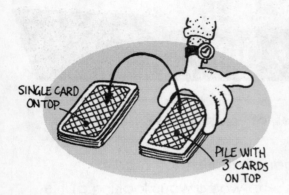

SINGLE CARD ON TOP

PILE WITH 3 CARDS ON TOP

4 Once this is done, pick up the pile with the three cards on top, and place it on top of the other pile. Your volunteer's favorite card is now in the middle of the deck.

5 Now look at your watch. Tell your audience that it is 17 minutes past 11, for example. Ask your volunteer to add these numbers together to get a total of 28. Then deal out the cards magically to reveal the favorite card is in fact the 28th card in the deck!

Oh my....
Will you just look at the time ...!
17 minutes past **11** !
17 + 11 = 28
Bet your card is **28**th down in the pack.

6 Of course, you can only use this trick when the time adds up to 28 – at 11:17, 12:16, 1:27, or 3.25, for example.

Trick 30
Cards that spell

★ **You need:** a deck of cards, a table

Prove to your audience that cards can spell their own number! This trick relies on the magician remembering the correct sequence when picking up the scattered cards.

1 You'll need to create a story explaining that you've discovered cards can actually spell, and you think spades (or whatever suit you choose) is the smartest suit.

2 Once you've selected your suit, take all 13 cards from that suit out of the deck. While doing this, randomly scatter the 13 cards face-up on a table. It is best if the cards are scattered widely across the table. It will seem less likely that you are going to pick up the cards in a particular order. Put the rest of the deck aside.

3 Now, pick the spade cards up in the following order: queen, 4, ace, 8, king, 2, 7, 5, 10, jack, 3, 6, 9. (Make sure the queen is at the top of the pack when it is face-down, and the 9 is on the bottom.)

4 Now all you have to do is have fun and remember how to spell!

5 Begin by spelling out A-C-E. When you say 'A', put the first card at the bottom of the pile. When you say 'C', put the second card at the bottom of the pile. When you say 'E', reveal the third card to be, the ace. This card is put to the side.

6 Next, spell T-W-O in the same way. Again when you get to the third card you will turn up the 2. Put it on top of the ace.

7 Continue spelling out T-H-R-E-E, F-O-U-R, F-I-V-E, etc. until the final card left is the king.

Trick 31
Find that card

★ **You need:** a sharp pencil, a pack of cards

In this trick, ask a volunteer to choose a card from the pack. After the volunteer returns the card to the pack, you'll "magically" locate it. This is a quick and effective trick that can be placed between two longer tricks for variety.

1 Lightly put a pencil line down one side of each card in the deck before the performance. This line needs to be dark enough for you to see, and light enough so no one in the audience sees it!

PENCIL LINE

2 Fan the deck of cards, face-down, toward a member of the audience. Ask him to select any card.

3 When the card is selected, ask your volunteer to show it to the audience. This is your opportunity to secretly turn the whole deck around.

4 Because the deck is reversed, the chosen card will be the only one with a pencil mark on the opposite side. With your eagle eyes, and your clever talk, it is an easy thing for you to cut the deck at the selected card, remove it with a flourish, and show it to the audience. Then, enjoy the applause!

The only card with a line on the other side.

Trick 32
Always red

★ **two decks of cards with different colored designs on the back (one design should be red), a piece of paper, a pen or pencil, a table**

As a magician it's great to involve your audience. In this trick, write a prediction on a piece of paper, and give it to an audience member. The prediction states: "You will pick the only red card out of the six cards". And that's what happens!

1 Pick out two specific cards for this trick. You'll need the six of either hearts or diamonds, and the other is the ace of spades or clubs. The ace is taken from the deck with the red design on the back, and the other five cards are from the other deck.

2 Besides from these two cards, the other four cards can be either clubs or spades, and any value from seven up.

3 Before your show, arrange the six chosen cards in the following order at the top of the pack: other, ace, six, other, other, other.

RED BACK

SIX OF DIAMONDS

4 Once the audience arrives, write your prediction on the paper in front of them, and show them. Ask for a volunteer. As she stands with you at the table, deal the top six cards, face-down, face-up, face-down, face-up, face-down, and face-up.

5 Now, the volunteer gives you a number between one and six, let's say she chooses four. Remember, you've predicted she will always choose a red card, so count from right to left, and you get to turn over the six of hearts or diamonds.

6 If the volunteer chooses one, pick up the ace and show the red-backed design. If they choose two, count from left to right, and show the ace again. For three, count from left to right, and pick up the six of hearts or diamonds. For five, count from right to left to pick up the ace. For six, pick up the six of diamonds or hearts right away.

7 Don't do this trick in front of the same audience. It becomes too obvious you knew what cards were where!

Trick 33
Your card is

★ **You need:** a deck of cards

This is another simple, but effective trick. Everyone will know you are a master or mistress of the cards! You will find the "selected" card hidden in the deck. Remember to deal the cards the same way every time.

1 Deal three piles with seven cards in each pile. Lay them out one, one, one, and two, two, two, rather than dealing one pile at a time. Put the remainder of the deck to one side, you won't need it.

2 Ask an audience member to pick a card from any pile, and memorize it, but don't tell anyone what it is. Then have him put the card back in the same pile.

3 Gather the three piles of cards, making sure the pile with the selected card is between the other two piles. Deal them out again, into three groups of seven cards.

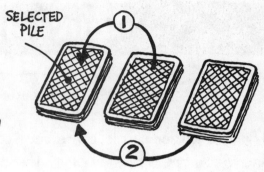

SELECTED PILE

4 Ask your volunteer to inspect each pile of cards, and tell you which pile the selected card is in now.

5 Again gather all the piles of cards, keeping the selected card's pile in the middle of the other two, and deal them out into three groups of seven.

6 The volunteer again finds his selected card, and indicates to you which pile it is in now. You gather the piles up, again keeping the selected card's pile in the middle of the other two.

Yes... I even amaze myself!

7 Spell out Y-O-U-R C-A-R-D I-S by removing a card for each letter. The next card is the selected card!

Trick 34
How odd

★ **You need:** a deck of cards, a table

This is a great trick to perform in front of young children. Many older children and adults realize you pick up an odd number of cards, but younger children probably won't. The trick works every time!

1 Spread the whole deck of cards out on a table, and ask a member of the audience to come forward to select as many cards as she wants, without actually looking at what she is doing. Once she's satisfied with her pile of cards, send her to one side of the stage area to count them.

2 While she is busy counting her cards, pick up a bunch of cards as casually as you can. The secret is that you always pick up an odd number of cards.

3 Now, tell your volunteer that whatever the number of cards in her hand, if it is an even number, your cards will make them odd. If she has an odd number, your cards will make them even.

4 Have her count her cards on to the table. Count with her so the audience can hear the final number too. Then, hand her your cards, and ask her to count all the cards again. The new total will be as you predicted.

5 There are two things to remember with this little trick. You need to practice casually scooping up an odd number of cards. This will make the trick work even better.

CHAPTER 2

Trick 35
Unfair deal

★ **You need:** a deck of cards, a table

Even though the cards for this trick are dealt out, and regathered while you—are not looking, you can still pick which card was selected. That's magic!

1 Before the performance, put all the 4s at the top of the deck, and all the 9s at the bottom of the deck. Practice shuffling so these eight cards stay where they are.

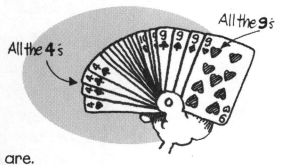

All the 4's

All the 9's

2 Fan the cards face-down and ask a member of your audience to select one card from the pack. While your volunteer is showing the card to the rest of the audience, but not letting you see which card it is, scoop up the remaining cards, and deal them into four equal piles of 13 (one pile will have one card less than the others).

3 Now, turn your back on the cards and the table, and ask your volunteer to place his chosen card on one of the piles. Then have him put each of the four piles of cards on top of the others in any order he likes. Have him hand the whole deck back to you.

4 Fan out the whole deck, and immediately pull the selected card from the fanned cards. How did you do it? Well, the secret is that once you deal the cards into four piles, there will be a 4 on top of each pile and a 9 on the bottom of each. When you fan out the cards, the selected card will be the card which is in between a 4, and a 9.

5 You don't have to use 4s and 9s, you can use any numbers you want, but don't use the face-cards. When several face-cards are next to each other, it is easier to see the trick.

Trick 36
Sticky hands

★ **You need:** a deck of cards, a ring, a toothpick, a table

This is another easy trick for young (and old!) magicians. It's easy to learn, easy to perform, and easy to make look good!

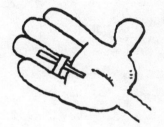

1 To get ready for this trick, put on the ring. Now, turn your palm so it's facing up. Slide the toothpick under the ring band.

2 Place your hand down on the table, making sure the audience doesn't see the toothpick. Tell the audience you are about to magically make the cards rise with just the palm of your hand.

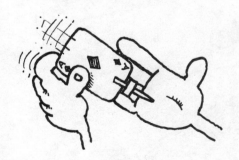

3 Take a card with your other hand, and slide it under the hand on the table. Do not pick your hand up from the table. Make sure the end of the card slides under the toothpick.

4 Pick up another card, and slide it under your hand from the other direction. This time slide it between your hand and the other end of the toothpick.

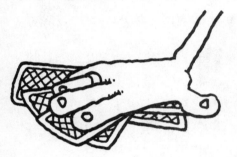

5 Try putting another four cards under your hand. They will be held in place by the original two cards.

6 Say your favorite magic phrase, such as "Abracadabra" or "Sim Sala Bim", and slowly lift your hand with the cards horizontally above the table. This is the time for some great acting by you! The cards stick to your hand, as if by magic!

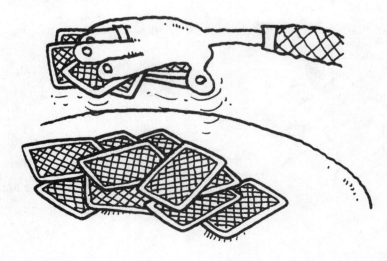

Trick 37
Gone! Into thin air

★ **You need:** a deck of cards, a handkerchief with a hem,
a toothpick, scissors, a table

So you've dazzled the audience by finding the cards they've
picked, but how about making cards disappear?
That is very cool...

1 A little bit of
preparation for this
trick is necessary. Make sure
the toothpick is as long as the
width of a playing card.
If it's too long, trim it. Now,
poke the toothpick into the
hem of the handkerchief until it is in the middle of that side.
You're ready for your audience!

2 Begin with a flourish by randomly spreading the deck
of cards on your table. Wave the handkerchief about,
and tell your audience you'll pick a card from the deck and
make it vanish into thin air.

3 Lay the handkerchief
over the cards so the
edge with the toothpick is
folded under the handkerchief.

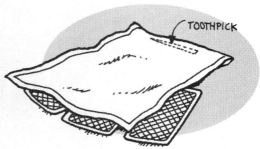

TOOTHPICK

4 Pick up the edge of the handkerchief by holding the toothpick between your thumb and index finger. It looks as if you are holding a card, right?

5 Say your favorite magic words, include something about making the card disappear. Throw the handkerchief into the air, and it appears the card has vanished!

Crafty Coin Puzzlers

Coins are easy to find around the house, so they are perfect for the budding magician to use in tricks. Of course, there are trick coins (double-headed and speciality) available at magic shops, but for most of the following tricks any coin will do!

Trick 38
Sleight of hand

★ **You need:** one coin

All magicians learn sleight of hand. Learn this trick well, and perform it at any time in any place—a show, a party, or even a restaurant!

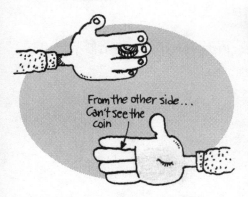

From the other side...
Can't see the coin

1 Begin by placing the coin firmly between the index and middle fingers of one hand. The coin should be hidden, so when *you* present your open hand (palm out) to the audience they can't see a thing.

2 Now we come to the part that you need to practice a lot. To produce the coin you turn your fingers in toward the palm of your hand, and use your thumb to bring the coin to the front.

Juliet...
Here art thou Romeo...

You're no Magician!!

Go away!

We want MAGIC!

Did you know?
By the 1800s, magic was often performed in theaters in many countries. In some places, magicians performed all the time.

Trick 39
Spin that coin

★ **You need:** a coin (with a textured edge), two pins, a table

This is a great trick, but you'll need to practice a lot to be able to hold the coin between the pins! If at first you don't succeed, keep trying! You'll get it!

1 Place the coin on the table and pick it up gently between the points of two pins.

2 Once you're sure it's secure, gently blow on the coin, and it will begin to spin.

3 That's all there is to it! It's a great trick to open a small magic show, you only need to keep the coin spinning for a few seconds, or longer if you like.

Trick 40
The coin through the table

★ You need: a coin, a table

In this trick, you'll make a coin magically pass through a table, from top to bottom. The trick relies on good sleight of hand and talking skills, so practice hard before the show. Your audience will think *you're* amazing!

1 First, hold up a coin and show it to your audience, so they can see it's a regular coin. Use some good magician's talk, explaining to them that you are going to push the coin through the table, but this is a hard trick, and it may take more than one attempt.

2 Now place the coin about 12 in. (30 cm) from the edge of the table. Using your right hand, slide the coin right to the edge of the table, and pick it up. Tap the coin on the table three times. Then hold the coin in the palm of your hand, and slap it down hard on the table, covering it with your hand.

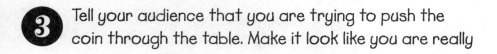

3 Tell your audience that you are trying to push the coin through the table. Make it look like *you are really*

pushing hard! Uncover the coin and look very disappointed, saying the trick has not worked.

4 Now tell your audience that you will try the trick one more time.

Once again slide the coin to the edge of the table with your right hand, but this time, secretly push it right off the table, and drop it into your left hand.

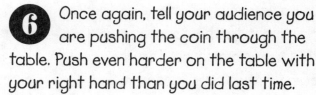

5 Reach under the table with your left hand and tap the bottom of the table with the coin, as you pretend to tap the coin on the tabletop with your right hand, so it sounds like the coin is still in your right hand. Do not let your audience see you have no coin in your right hand!

Well... Will you look at that! It looks like a coin to me!

6 Once again, tell your audience you are pushing the coin through the table. Push even harder on the table with your right hand than you did last time.

7 Finally, use your right hand to reach under the table and take the coin from your left hand. Bring the coin up and show it to the audience. Hey Presto! The coin has passed through the table!

Trick 41
The coin fold

★ **You need:** a coin, a small piece of paper

Another easy but effective trick using just one coin is fantastic for a small audience.

1 Place the coin in the center of a piece of paper.

2 Fold the bottom edge of the paper up and over the coin, leaving a 0.25 in. (6 mm) gap between the two edges of the paper.

3 Fold the right edge of the paper back behind the coin.

4 Then fold the left edge of the paper back behind the coin.

85

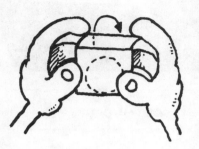

5 Make the final fold by bending the top flap of the paper back behind the coin. It seems as if the coin is completely wrapped, but in fact the top edge is still open.

6 You now turn the package around so the open edge allows the coin to slip into the palm of your hand, where it stays while you "prove" the coin is gone. Tear up the paper package. *Voilà!* The coin has disappeared.

Did you know?

Harry Houdini (Ehrich Weiss was his real name) is still the best known magician. He was known as an escapologist, and he was known to say "No Jail Could Hold Him!" He often performed outdoors, which added to the drama. He escaped from a straightjacket, while hanging by his ankles tied high above a street. He received plenty of publicity for that trick!

CHAPTER 3

Trick 42
A pocket full of change

★ **You need:** a handful of coins, a black marker

Be sure to wear a pair of jeans or pants with pockets in them for this trick.

You'll have a volunteer choose and mark a coin for you, from a handful of loose change. Then you will make the chosen coin disappear from your hand and reappear in your pocket with the rest of the coins!

1 First, remove a handful of change from your left pocket, and show it to your audience, using your left hand. Have a volunteer choose a coin and mark it with an "X". Then ask her to return it to your hand, with the other coins.

Keep the MARKED COIN in your left hand

2 Now pretend to pick up the marked coin with your right hand, but do not take the coin. Secretly cover it with the other coins, so the audience cannot see it. Hold your closed right hand in the air, so the audience thinks the coin is in it.

3 Put the coins in your left hand back in your pocket, but wait for a moment so the audience is convinced the marked coin (which is now covered by other coins) is not in it.

ABRACADABRA!

4 Take your closed right hand and make a large circle in the air, saying the magic words, "Abracadabra!" Then slap your closed right hand on your left leg 3 times, just below the pocket.

5 Show your audience that your right hand is now empty and tell them the marked coin returned to your pocket.

6 Take out the handful of loose change and ask your volunteer to find her marked coin. Of course, it will be there. Wow, incredible!

AHHRR! The COIN!

You'll have to agree... That's no ordinary loose change!

I HAVEN'T GOT TIME FOR MAGIC I'M TOO BUSY DRIVING ROUND THE UNIVERSE!

Did you know?
Popular magicians took their travelling shows around the world. Early in the twentieth century, one American magician had his Wonder Show of the Universe touring the world. He was America's top performer for 30 years.

3
CHAPTER

Trick 43

Where's that coin?

★ **You need:** a handkerchief, a coin, Blu-Tack, a table

In this trick, a coin is placed in the center of a handkerchief in full view of an audience. The magician weaves a magic spell—and it's gone!

1 Before facing your audience, stick a small piece of Blu-Tack to one corner of the handkerchief. This needs to be kept hidden from the audience at all times during the performance.

2 Spread the handkerchief out on the table, but still hold onto the corner with the Blu-Tack. Place the coin in the center of the handkerchief. Immediately cover it with the Blu-Tack corner.

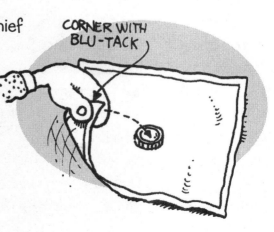

CORNER WITH BLU-TACK

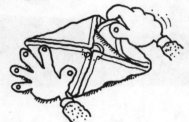

3 Fold the other three corners into the center of the handkerchief over the coin.

4 Place the fingers of both hands under the folded edge of the handkerchief, which is nearest you. Because of this quick move the coin, stuck to the handkerchief, ends up in your hand.

5 Show both sides of the handkerchief to the audience, give it a quick shake and put it in your pocket to finish. Or pretend to blow your nose on it, or pretend to sneeze, and cover your nose and mouth with it—anything for a good finale and a round of applause!

6 Perhaps you would like to make this coin reappear? It can be done, by magic! Or it's good planning. Simply have an identical coin hidden somewhere. When you remove the coin from the handkerchief, keep it in your hand, and produce it from anywhere you like. Maybe from behind one of your audience member's ear?

Great...I need a hanky to blow my nose!

Trick 44
The chemical coin

★ **You need:** one coin, a table, a chair

You'll also need a good story, and it's best to perform this intriguing trick before a small audience.

1 Your story should begin as soon as the audience arrives. Talk excitedly about what you've just read on the Internet—that chemicals in the human body can degrade the metals in a coin. In fact, coins can just disappear!

2 Show the coin to your audience, and sit down at your table resting your chin on your right hand. Rub the coin in your left hand against your right forearm. Make sure no one can see the coin as you do this.

3 While you rub the coin on your arm, continue the fantastic story you began. Now, the coin should slip from your left hand, and drop on to the table. Continue with the story, and make sure you are looking at your audience.

4 Pick up the coin in your right hand, and pretend to pass it back to your left hand, but keep it in your right hand.

5 Prop up your chin in your right hand, and pretend to rub the coin on your forearm as before. Do this masterfully, and continue with your story.

6 Keep rubbing for a little longer. Then, suddenly look a little concerned. Continue to rub, maybe even a little harder, and slowly stop rubbing. Lift the fingers of your left hand one at a time.

At the same time, carefully drop the coin into your shirt. Then, with a flourish, show your audience the coin has disappeared. Take a bow!

3
CHAPTER

Trick 45
Holey napkin

★ **You need:** a coin, a cloth napkin, a black marker

This is a very impressive trick—easy to do, and great to watch!

1 Your audience must be seated in front of you, as with most tricks! Ask a volunteer for a coin, or hand over yours. Ask the volunteer to mark it with the marker, so it will be recognizable later on.

2 Hold the coin upright between your thumb and index finger of your left hand.

3 Place the napkin over your hand, so the coin is in the center of the napkin.

4 Now for the tricky part—carefully arrange a small fold of the napkin between your thumb and the coin. With your right hand, lift the front of the napkin, and drape it back over the top of the napkin, and over your left wrist.

COIN
FOLD

5 Show your audience the coin is still there.

COIN

6 Continue to hold both the coin and the napkin. Then, flick your left wrist forward to make both halves of the napkin fall forward.

7 Now, twist the napkin so it appears the coin is wrapped securely inside. Place a little pressure on the edge of the coin, and it should rise magically up through the napkin, or that is how it will appear to your audience!

CHAPTER 3

Trick 46
The coin tells

★ **You need:** four coins of different values, a table

You'll be amazed at how simple this trick is. Don't forget some good stories so your audience is really convinced it's magic!

1 Place the four coins on the table while talking about telepathy. Ask an audience member to choose a coin while your back is turned. Tell her to hold it tightly, and concentrate hard so you can pick up the vibes from her mind!

2 Silently concentrate for a few moments. Pretend you are trying to pick up thought-waves, but what you're really doing is slowly counting to 30.

3 When you reach 30, sadly say that you aren't receiving any thoughts from her. Tell her to concentrate harder. Whatever she says, ask for the coin to be put back on the table while you're still not looking, and say that you'll get the coins to tell you which one was selected.

4 Turn around, and pick up each coin. Hold it up to your ear to "hear" the coins "talking" to you. What you're really doing is feeling each coin, because the one which was held by your volunteer will be much warmer than the others.

5 So, once you find the warmest coin, show it to the audience, and wait for the applause!

Trick 47

The weeping coin

> ★ **You need:** a coin, a small piece of wet (but not dripping) sponge

An emotional, crying coin? Now, I've seen it all!

SPONGE

1 Before your audience arrives, wet the small piece of sponge, and make sure it fits between the coin and your thumb without being seen. It must hold enough water to allow you to make the coin "cry".

2 In front of your audience, hold the coin between your thumb and index finger (keeping the wet sponge hidden with your thumb). Tell them a really good story about how some coins are very emotional, and you can get this one to cry!

3 Pretend to tell a really sad story. As you're telling the story, squeeze the sponge gently. "Tears" will begin to flow!

OH...! WHAT A SAD LITTLE COIN! DID I MAKE YOU CRY?

4 Once the tears stop, put the sponge and coin in your pocket. If a member of the audience wants to see if the coin is real, pull out the coin, minus the sponge.

Trick 48
Snatch!

★ You need: a coin

Again, a simple coin trick which makes the magician look very, very clever! The idea is to put a coin in the palm of your hand and challenge a volunteer to snatch it from you before you can close your hand. Your volunteer can't do it, but when you switch places, you get the coin on your first try.

1 Put the coin on your palm and keep it flat.

2 Your volunteer now tries to grab the coin before you close your hand—be as quick as you can. Your volunteer will fail every time.

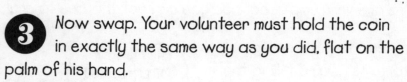

3 Now swap. Your volunteer must hold the coin in exactly the same way as you did, flat on the palm of his hand.

4 How do you do it? Place your fingers and thumb together, without touching. Make sure your fingers are pointing down toward the coin.

5 Quickly move your hand down, gently striking the palm of your volunteer's hand with your fingertips. This will make your volunteer's hand to be pushed downward a little. The coin will jump up into your waiting fingers! Try it! It works!

Classic Conjuring

Every magician needs to spend some time
perfecting a few classic magic tricks. Don't worry
if some of the tricks seem old, or so well known
you think everyone knows them. It's what you say,
and how you perform them that your friends will
love. You'll probably think of a new way to do at
least one of them anyway. That's OK, magic
doesn't stay the same.

Trick 49
Long arm

★ **You need:** nothing–just your arm!

Perhaps not a classic trick, but a classic effect. People love seeing a magician do something, they don't think they can do themselves...

1 You'll need to practice this trick over and over again. Try doing it in front of a mirror, so you can see the effect youself. You do need to wear a jacket or a coat while performing (and practicing) this trick.

2 First, stand still and bend your arm so your left hand and wrist is level with your waist.

3 Now, gently pinch the loose skin on the back of your left hand, near the knuckle of the middle finger, with the other hand.

4
CHAPTER

4 Shake this skin a little. It appears you're actually stretching your arm by tugging it out of your sleeve to an abnormal length. That's all there is to this trick, but it's so effective when done really well and with a great story, for example: "The guy you met in Long Beach...boy, did he have a long reach!"

PRESS SLEEVE AGAINST YOU HERE

5 Once you've pulled out your really long arm, you can tap your arm back into the jacket sleeve as part of the story.

6 The effect is created by hugging the jacket or coat sleeve tightly to your body as you move your arm. Don't let the audience see your elbow, or you'll give the trick away!

Trick 50

Where's my thumb?

★ **You need:** just your hands

This trick takes much longer to read through, than do!
But you'll need to practice it for several weeks before
performing it. You want your audience to believe the tip of
your left thumb is being magically removed.

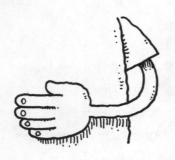

1 Begin by holding your left hand
in front of you, at about your
waist. The palm of your hand faces
toward you, your fingers are flat,
and pointing to the right. Make sure
your thumb is on the same line as your
index finger.

2 Pretend to pull the
top off your left
thumb with your right thumb
and index finger. Make a big
deal of this with lots of
grunts, groans, and twisted facial
expressions! Of course, you can't
do it, can you?

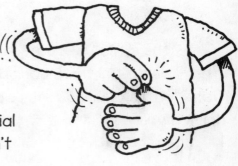

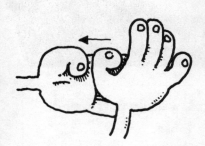

3 Well maybe you can! Try again, and this time, as you place your right index finger over the left thumb, bend the top of your left thumb down, and put your right thumb underneath the index finger so it looks like a complete thumb.

4 Tuck the other fingers of your right hand away, so the audience can clearly see your right thumb. It looks as if it is your left thumb tip! Got it? Good!

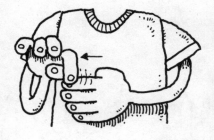

5 To complete the illusion, keep your left hand still and slowly slide the right thumb along the top of your left index finger. Then, slowly slide it back to its original spot.

6 When your thumbs touch, bring back the fingers which were screening the join and show your hands with thumbs intact to your audience! Take a bow!

Trick 51
Silky hanky

★ **You need:** a small rubber band, a large patterned silk square, a ring, a table

This is a simple trick you can do practically anywhere—great for entertaining young children and adults alike! Show them you can make a ring disappear!

1 Before facing your audience, slip a rubber band over three of the fingers on your left hand.

2 Once your audience arrives, take out your silk hanky, and wave it around using your right hand so all eyes are on it, and not on the rubber band over your fingers! You don't want your audience to notice the rubber band.

3 Spread the hanky over your left hand with a flourish, and secretly slip your thumb into the rubber band to widen it more.

CHAPTER 4

4 Ask your audience if you can borrow a ring (of course, if they haven't got one, you already happen to have one on your table!).

5 Show everyone the ring. Then, place it on the silk hanky above the rubber band. With your free hand, rub the ring saying a magic chant. Of course, what you are doing is pushing the ring through the band into a fold of silk below.

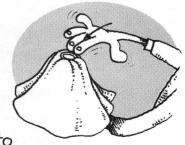

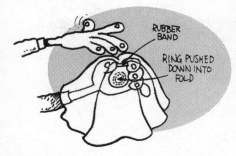

RUBBER BAND

RING PUSHED DOWN INTO FOLD

6 Slip the band off your fingers to trap the ring in a fold in the silk while making a dramatic gesture, and saying more magic words.

7 Dramatically whip the hanky away with your right hand, and look amazed to see that the ring is gone.

RING IN FOLD

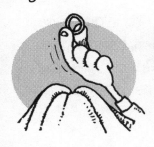

8 Return the ring by spreading the silk over your left hand again. Reach into the folds with your right hand, and pull out the ring with a smile!

Trick 52
The Smallest Magic Wand

★ **You need:** A pair of scissors, a matchbox, 21 matches, glue, a coin, a table.

You will amaze your audience with this trick, by using "the smallest magic wand in the world" to turn matches into money!

1 Prepare the matchbox before the show. Ask an adult to help you with this. Carefully cut 20 matches in half, with the scissors. Then glue all the top halves of the matches into one end of the matchbox. Wait for the glue to dry.

WHOLE MATCH

MATCHES

GLUED MATCHES

When the glue is dry, you will see that if you open the box halfway, it looks like you have a regular box of matches. Now put a coin inside the other end of the matchbox. Finally, put a whole match in, on top of the glued half-matches.

2 When your audience arrives, hold up the matchbox. Open it halfway and show them the matches.

3 Now is the time to use some good magician's talk. Tell your audience you are going to use special powers to create the world's smallest magic wand. Then you'll use your new wand to make money!

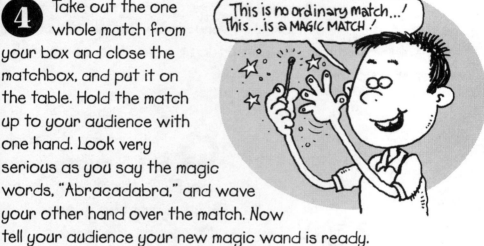

4 Take out the one whole match from your box and close the matchbox, and put it on the table. Hold the match up to your audience with one hand. Look very serious as you say the magic words, "Abracadabra," and wave your other hand over the match. Now tell your audience your new magic wand is ready.

This is no ordinary match...! This...is a MAGIC MATCH!

5 Tap the matchbox lightly with the your magic wand. Once again say the magic words, "Abracadabra." Then open the other end of the matchbox to reveal the coin inside. Hold the matchbox up to your audience, so they can see the coin. Say something like, "Presto! Money from matches!"

6 Take the coin out of the matchbox and give it to a member of your audience, so they can see it is real and not stuck inside the box. Wow! Amazing!

Trick 53
The classic scarf trick

★ **You need:** a long silky scarf, a high-necked top

Most of the classic tricks are very simple, just like this one. The real trick for a magician, young or old, is to be smooth and professional!

1 Prepare for this trick by tucking the silky scarf into the neck of your shirt in front, so it looks like it's around your neck.

2 In front of your audience, hold the ends of the scarf, and pull both ends forward on the count of three, or perhaps while chanting "Sim Sala Bim!"

3 Pull the scarf forward in one quick motion, so it appears to pass straight through your neck! Magic!

Did you know?

Harry Houdini died after a student, who had heard he could withstand a powerful blow to the stomach, punched Houdini before he was ready. He was taken to hospital, and died a few days later.

Trick 54

The magic cone

★ **You need: a paper cone with a secret pocket, a silk hanky**

It's worth finding a special cone, or making your own for this trick. It's likely to be one of the best tricks you do. Tell your audience you will make a silk hanky disappear.

SECRET POCKET

1 Unfold the cone so your audience can see it's just a cone (but we know better!) with one decorated side, and one plain side.

SECRET POCKET

2 Fold it back into a cone, and push the silk hanky into the secret pocket.

3 Speak some magic words and clap your hands together, flattening the cone, and the silk in the pocket!

4 Carefully, unfold the cone and show there is nothing on the front or back of it. The hanky is gone!

Trick 55
How eggstraordinary!

> ★ **You need:** an uncooked egg, a pencil,
> a silk handkerchief, a teaspoon, a large sewing needle,
> an egg cup (optional), a table

Done well, with lots of clever chat, this trick will make your audience truly believe you can pull a handkerchief out of an egg.

1 Prepare the egg before the show. Ask an adult to help you with this. Carefully make a small hole in one end of the egg using the needle. Then make a larger hole, big enough to poke the pencil through, in the other end of the egg. Now gently blow into the smaller hole. The contents of the egg will come out

of the larger hole. Carefully wash the inside of the shell, and let it dry naturally. Once the shell is dry, use the pencil to carefully poke your silk hanky into the larger hole.

2 Now for the best part! Pretend that you are going to make breakfast. Show the egg to the audience, but keep the holes out of sight by placing your thumb and

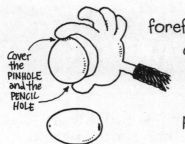

Cover the PINHOLE and the PENCIL HOLE

forefinger over them. Just as you are about to break the egg, pretend you are going to sneeze. With the egg in your hands, cover your nose. Then, pretend the sneeze went away.

3 Now put the egg on the table, be sure to hide the holes, and gently tap it with the teaspoon. Then gasp, and saysomething like, "How eggstraordinary! You'll never guess what I've found!"

4 Excitedly break the egg apart, and pull out the hanky!

OH GREAT! I was going to make a rabbit disappear from this hat, but it's already DISAPPEARED!

Trick 56
Palming

★ **You need:** three small sponge balls – you can buy these at all good magic and novelty shops. You can also shop for magician's props on the Internet! Many magic shops have websites. Ask an adult to help you look them up.

To do this trick, you'll need to learn a new skill—it's called palming.

1 First, you need to learn to palm the sponge balls. Good thing they aren't very large! Place one ball in the palm of your hand. Bring your thumb over a little to hold it in position. It shouldn't move, even when you hold your hand upright. Practice until you can keep the sponge ball in place when you are moving your hands around a lot. Now try to palm two balls!

2 Once you are really good at palming, you're ready to move on to the next step, tricking your audience!

3 Have all three sponges in your pocket before you begin your show. Tell the audience you are getting two sponge balls out of your pocket. Show the audience the two sponges in your right hand.

However, you have already palmed a ball, so there are really three sponge balls in your right hand, but the audience can see only two of them.

4 Tell the audience you are moving one to your left hand. When you move the ball, secretly move the third ball to your left hand too.

5 Now, hold two sponge balls up in the air, one in each hand, and ask your audience to agree that you have one ball in each hand. Then, pass the ball from your right hand to your left hand, saying as you do: "Now I have two sponge balls in my left hand."

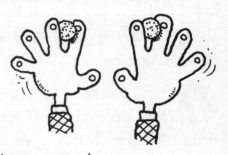

6 But there are three balls nestling in your hand.

7 Palming skills will be very handy throughout your magic career. Learn to do it well!

OF COURSE IT'S A REAL GRENADE... EVERYTHING IS **REAL** IN MAGIC!

Did you know?
During the Second World War, many magicians entertained the troops. Magicians traveled overseas, as well as performing at home.

4
CHAPTER

Trick 57

Together forever!

★ **You need:** a five dollar bill, two paper clips

This is another great trick. Tell your audience you can make two paper clips link up without touching them.

1 Stand directly in front of your audience, and fold the five dollar bill into a Z shape.

2 Place one paper clip on the first fold.
Place the second clip on the second fold.

3 Hold up the five dollar bill so the audience can see what it looks like. Then, warn the front row of the audience they may have to duck!

4 Now, carefully hold the five dollar bill at each end, and quickly snap it back into a straightened position. The paper clips will link themselves together, and possibly fly right out into the audience!

5 Stand by for loud applause.

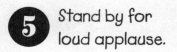

Trick 58

The spinning egg

★ **You need:** eleven fresh eggs,
one hard-boiled egg, a table

Whatever you do, don't drop any of the fresh eggs!

1 Prepare for the trick by hard-boiling an egg. When the egg cools, place it back in the egg carton, making sure you remember where you put it.

2 Once you are in front of your audience, pass out the eggs to eleven volunteers in the audience, keeping the hard-boiled one for yourself.

3 Using your egg, show them how to spin an egg. Obviously, you need to practice first!

4 Then, invite the eleven volunteers up one-by-one to spin their eggs. *No one will be able to do this little trick because a fresh egg won't spin.*

5 You could also try having two hard-boiled eggs in the carton, because then one of the volunteers will be able to spin an egg, and you can make a really big deal out of the fact that they have *magic powers* too!

CHAPTER 4

Trick 59
Cups and balls

★ **You need:** three cups, four small sponge balls,
one larger sponge ball

It is an old magic trick to hide a ball under a cup!
Magicians all over the world learn it to entertain, and
confuse their audiences.

The special cups used in this trick can be purchased
wherever magic props are sold; consider buying a set of
clear plastic cups to begin with, so you can see exactly
where each ball is as you learn. Each cup has a rim which
prevents another cup from being pushed inside it. The ball
can be hidden in the space created. Also, the bottom of
each cup has an indent which allows a soft sponge ball to
rest without rolling off.

1 To prepare, place
the large ball in
your left pocket, one
small ball in each of the
three cups, and the
fourth small ball in your
left hand. Stack the
cups inside each other.

117

2 When you begin the trick, turn each cup over quickly, keeping the ball hidden underneath.

3 Wave your hand over all the cups. Then, lift the right-hand one (with your right hand) showing a ball resting on the table underneath it. Transfer the cup to your left hand, so it covers the small ball hidden there.

4 Repeat with the other two cups, showing the two other balls, and sitting the cups on top of the one already in your left hand.

5 Now place each cup mouth-down directly behind each ball on the table. First place one to the right and then the left, so the first cup now becomes the central cup. As you place

 this cup on the table, make sure the concealed ball drops into it as you turn it upside down.

6 Pick up one of the balls, and place it on top of the central cup. Next, place the other cups on top. With a wave of your hand, lift all three cups as one to reveal a ball on the table. To the audience, it appears you have magically made the ball pass through the base of the cup. But wait, there's more!

7 Again, separate the cups and place them mouth-down on the table. This time put the cup which contains the extra ball in the middle over the ball already on the table. Place a ball on top of this cup and repeat step 6. The difference could be that you invite an audience member to wave their hand over the cup. Take the large ball from your pocket, and hold it in your left hand.

8 Lift all three cups as one and, astonishingly, all three small balls are on the table. Casually place the cups over your left hand. Place all three cups (and the larger ball) on the table and act as though the trick is finished.

9 A bit of acting here will earn you loud applause, so hesitate as if you want to tell your audience something, but shouldn't. Then say you'll reveal a magic secret, you did use more than three balls for the trick! Pick up the cups to reveal the larger ball.

THANKYOU! THANKYOU! THANKYOU!

Masterly Mental Magic

A magician can gain much by learning a few mentally challenging tricks. They always work, and always make a magician look, well, magical! Many are card tricks, many need a little preparation. Of course, they all need practice, but it's worth the trouble, because they are all terrific tricks.

101 COOL MAGIC TRICKS

5
CHAPTER

Trick 60
Colors in your life

★ **You need:** six index cards, a black marker, a table

Keep the audience's attention on the great names of colors you choose to distract them from the simplicity of this trick!

1 A little preparation is needed for this trick. Write the name of a different color on each index card. Be creative with the names of the colors, because you have to have a different number of letters for each color.

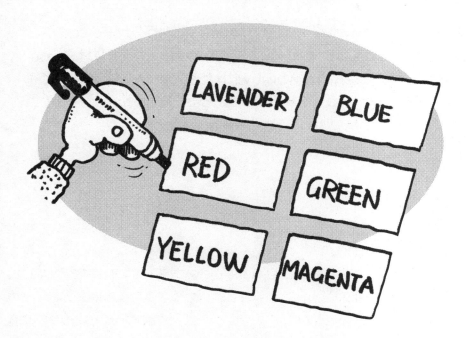

2 Perhaps you would have red (3) and blue (4), green (5), and yellow (6). These are fairly straightforward colors, but how about magenta (7) and finally, lavender (8 letters).

3 Now, you're ready for your audience. Place the cards randomly on a table with the names of the colors facing up and ask a volunteer to pick a color.

4 Your volunteer should not tell anyone the name of the color, but must silently spell the name of the color, one letter at a time, as you touch each card. When your volunteer reaches the last letter of the color, he must say "Stop", and your hand will be resting on the correct card!

5 How it works? Well, for the first two letters you touch any card at all. Then, with the third letter you touch the three-letter word, with the fourth letter the four-letter word, and so on. You will always be on the correct card when the audience member says stop!

Trick 61
Whacky clock

★ **You need:** a photocopy of a large clock, a pencil

Find a really great clock face to photocopy, because the more crazy-looking it is, the more it will distract your audience from this simple, but clever trick.

1 Ask a volunteer to look at the photocopied clock face, and select a number from it— silently! Ask your volunteer to add 1 to the number she selects. If she chooses 7, she adds 1 to make 8, keeping this all in her head.

2 If she needs to write down the number she first thought of, let her do so, but make sure you can't see it.

3 Now for the clever part! Ask your volunteer to begin counting silently from her current number (so the next number is 9). Each time you tap your pencil on the clock's face.

123

4 When she gets to 20, she should say "stop!" You will be on the correct number. Circle it on the clock's face, and hand it face-down to your volunteer. Have her tell the audience the number she originally selected, and then turn over the page to reveal your answer. Your answer will be correct every time!

ANTI-CLOCKWISE FROM 6

5 The secret? Well, you tap on the clock's face at the number 6 each time you do the trick, and you tap counter-clockwise on the numbers. When your volunteer says stop after reaching 20, you will always be on the correct number. It's magic!

6 If you are going to repeat this trick in front of the same audience, make sure no one sees where you begin tapping.

5
CHAPTER

Trick 62
Plus and minus

★ **You need:** a piece of paper, a pencil

If your mathematics skills are good, this is an easy one. You can't use a calculator—it just doesn't look as impressive!

1 Ask a member of your audience to write down a five figure number on a piece of paper. The number must be made up of five different numbers. No two numbers can be the same. Your volunteer keeps the piece of paper, and his math hidden from you at all times. For example, the number might be: 36412.

2 Now ask him to reverse the number, and write it underneath the first number. subtract the second number from the first.

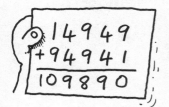

3 Have your volunteer reverse this number, and write it down underneath the previous number. This time add them together.

④ Once he has the answer, you need to act up a storm, saying you can read his mind. It will almost always be 109,890. Occasionally, it will be 99,099. If you are wrong on the first guess of 109,890, blame it on bad vibes and say, "Ah, it's coming to me now. It's 99,099!"

Trick 63
Famous names

> ★ **You need:** ten cards big enough to write names on but small enough to fit into the magic hat, a pencil, a piece of paper, a hat

You'll choose the correct name every time, but you can only do this trick one time in front of each audience!

1 Ask people in your audience to call out ten famous names. And as they do, write each name on a card and place it in the hat. Well, that's what your audience thinks you're doing! What you are really doing is repeatedly writing down the first name called, perhaps it was Nelson Mandela. Write that on a card, place it in the hat, and pretend to write down the next nine names called out—maybe you'll hear Britney Spears, Brad Pitt, Shakespeare, or Abraham Lincoln shouted out. But every time write down Nelson Mandela (the first name), and put the card in the hat!

2 Now it's easy. Ask someone from the audience to come up and pick a name out of the hat. Read it, but don't tell anyone.

3 Ask your volunteer to concentrate hard on the name. You do the same. Make sure you act as if you are concentrating very hard! After a few seconds of this, tell the audience you believe you can read your volunteer's mind, and the answer is "Nelson Mandela."

4 Everyone will be amazed, and cheer wildly. Never repeat this trick with the same audience. It is too easy to figure out!

Trick 64
Mystery mathematics

> ★ **You need:** a piece of paper, a pencil

You'll amaze your audience with your superior number skills. You just remember one thing.

1 Ask an audience member to call out a single digit number (a number from 1 to 9). Write it on a piece of paper, and show it to the audience.

2 Now, take that number, double it, add 4, then divide by 2, and finally subtract the original number. For example, if the number called out was 3; double it to get 6; add 4 to get 10; divide by 2 and get 5; subtract 3, and the answer is 2.

3 Ready to predict the answer? Once an adding number has been chosen, the answer will always be half of that number. In the above example, you added 4. Immediately you know the answer is 2. You can make it look even better if you ask an audience member to shout out an adding number. Just remember the answer will always be half of that number.

4 Change the adding number a few more times— this is one trick where the audience rarely guesses how the trick works!

Trick 65
They match!

★ **You need:** two pieces of paper, two pencils

With this cool trick, your volunteer is in on the secret!
Tell the audience that your mental powers are so good
that you can write the same sentence as someone from
the audience!

1 Ask a volunteer to write down a sentence on one
piece of paper. It can be anything your volunteer likes.
Then ask your volunteer to fold the paper and hand it to
another member of the audience.

2 Put the other piece of
paper in front of you,
and tell the audience you will
write the same sentence.
This is the time to use your
acting skills as you pretend to
be concentrating hard. Write
down "You're right, they
match!" on your piece of paper.
Fold it, and hand it to the same
person who is holding the
sentence, written by the
volunteer.

3 Ask this person to open the volunteer's piece of paper, and read the sentence out loud.

4 Now ask the same person to open the paper containing your sentence, and read it out loud. The reader will laugh (of course!) and say, "You're right, they match!"

5 You audience will be amazed, and you'll get lots of applause!

Trick 66

Secrets? What secrets?

★ **You need:** two pieces of paper, a pen or pencil

People who use calculators to do their math may find this trick hard. You need to do your math on paper, unless you can find a calculator that has room for a ten-digit answer!

1 Begin by asking for a volunteer to help you with this trick.

2 Give him a piece of paper, and a pen or pencil, and tell him he is going to be a human calculations. Then, just by looking at these calculations, you will be able to tell the volunteer's phone number and age!

3 First of all the volunteer writes down his phone number on the paper, then multiplies it by two (see the example). Now ask him to do the following: add five to the total, then multiply it by 50, add his age, add 365 and finally subtract 615.

$$
\begin{array}{r}
9287915 \\
\times\ 2 \\
\hline
18575830 \\
\end{array}
$$

$$
\begin{array}{r}
18575830 \\
+\ 5 \\
\hline
18575835 \\
\end{array}
$$

$$\begin{array}{r} 18575835 \\ \times\ 50 \\ \hline 928791750 \end{array}$$

$$\begin{array}{r} 928791750 \\ +\ 49 \\ \hline 928791799 \end{array}$$

$$\begin{array}{r} 928791799 \\ +\ 365 \\ \hline 928792164 \end{array}$$

$$\begin{array}{r} 928792164 \\ -\ 615 \\ \hline 9287915/49 \end{array}$$

4 The last two numbers in the above sequence "49" represent the volunteer's age, and the other numbers are his phone number. Of course, if the second to last number is 0, your volunteer is under 10 years old, and only the last number represents his age.

5 This trick is very effective if you can remember the sequence of instructions without referring to this book or your notes. Don't repeat the trick for the same group. Once will leave them guessing.

You're going to have to move close to the screen to see this one. I'll turn this little FLEA into a DUST MITE!

Did you know?
After television was invented, people began to stay home more. Magicians wanting to perform successfully on this new medium had to create smaller, cleverer tricks.

Trick 67
Super Sweet Numbers!

★ **You need:** a bowl of sugar cubes, a pencil, a glass of water, a table

---

Plenty of practice and good talking skills will help *you* perform this popular trick.

1 Place the bowl of sugar cubes and glass of water on the table, in front of your audience. Have a volunteer choose a number between 1 and 10. Write the number on one of the sugar cubes with a pencil (be sure to write it well, so the number stands out).

2 Show the sugar cube to your audience. Then hold it between *your* thumb and finger for a moment, with the number facing your thumb, pressing hard. The number will transfer onto your thumb while you are pressing! Now drop the sugar cube into the glass of water and let it dissolve.

3 Hold your volunteer's hand above the glass. Tell *your* audience you will use *your* mental powers to make the number appear on her hand. Be sure to press your thumb into the palm of your volunteer's hand. The number will then transfer from your thumb to her palm.

4 Say the magic words, "Sim Sala Bim!" Lift your volunteer's hand and show the audience. They will be amazed to see the number on her palm!

Trick 68
Dinky dice

★ **You need:** three dice, a pen, a piece of paper, a table

When performing this great trick, a smart magician must remember that the opposite sides of a dice always add up to seven.

1 Use a lot of drama when performing this trick, because the trick really does itself. Show the audience the three dice, the pen, and the paper. Ask for a volunteer to help you.

2 Stand at the back of the stage with your back to the audience. Ask your volunteer to roll the dice, pick them up in any order, and stack them one on top of the other.

3 Keep your back to the audience, and ask your volunteer to carefully add up the numbers of the five hidden faces of the dice. The volunteer should write the answer, and silently show it to the audience.

4 Once the audience has seen the paper with the number on it, the volunteer should tear it up. Now, turn around and face the audience. Move to the table and stare at the stacked dice.

5 Bring your hands to your head and pretend you are concentrating. Announce the correct answer to amaze your audience.

6 The secret to this trick is that the opposite sides of a dice always add up to seven. You have three dice, so 7 multiplied by 3 equals 21. When you turn, and step forward, look at the number on the top die, let's say it is a 5. Take 5 away from 21, and get 16. Tell your audience that 16 is the number on the piece of paper. You're absolutely correct.

$7 \times 3 = 21$

5 ON TOP

$21 - 5 = 16$

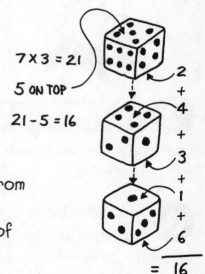

$$\begin{aligned} & 2 \\ + & 4 \\ + & 3 \\ + & 1 \\ + & 6 \\ \hline = & 16 \end{aligned}$$

7 Stand with your back to the audience, and have the volunteer tear up the paper. Act as if you are struggling with the answer. The answer is right in front of you all the time!

Trick 69
Magic dates

★ **You need:** a pen, a piece of paper, an envelope,
a calculator (optional)

This simple, but intriguing trick only requires the magician to know what year it is! Read all the way through this trick first!

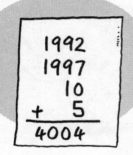

```
  1992
  1997
    10
+    5
  4004
```

1 Write a number on a piece of paper, and place it in the envelope. Seal it, and ask for a volunteer to help with the trick. (See Step 6 for which number to write down.)

2 When the volunteer comes forward, give him the sealed envelope, and ask him to keep it in his pocket until you ask for it.

3 Give the volunteer the paper and pen, and ask him to write down, then add up, the following four numbers:

- ๏ the year he was born
- ๏ the year he began school
- ๏ the age he'll be at the end of this year
- ๏ the number of years since he started school

4 For example, the numbers might look like this:

```
  1992
  1997
    10
 +  5
 ─────
  4004
```

5 When the volunteer
has finished the
addition, ask him to open
the envelope. He will be
amazed to find that
you already wrote the
answer that is sealed
in the envelope!

6 The secret is to remember
the current year! Double the current year
to always be right!

7 If you ask an adult volunteer some questions, you can
replace "the year he or she began school", and "the
number of years since he or she started school" with either
"the year he or she began working" and "the number of years
since he or she began working", or "the year he or she got
married" and "the number of years since he or she got
married". The answer will always be the same—the current
year doubled.

5

CHAPTER

Trick 70
Old timers' card trick

★ **You need:** a deck of cards

This is a trick which "works itself" but you need to keep up the entertaining patter—so practise telling your story before unleashing this on your audience.

1 Take any three cards from a full deck of cards, so you now have 49 cards in your hand.

2 Ask a member of the audience to select any card from the deck, memorize it, and put it back in the deck. Then, shuffle the deck thoroughly. Now, hold the cards face-down, and ask your volunteer to deal the cards into seven piles face-up, dealing across the rows each time.

3 Stand far away as your volunteer does this. Then ask your volunteer to search each pile until she finds the card she memorized. Numbering the piles from the left to right, ask her to tell you the number of the pile the card is in.

Once you have this information, ask her to put the piles on top of each other. Put the second pile on top of the first, the third on top of both, the fourth on top, and so on.

4 When all the piles are together, ask your volunteer to deal the cards face-down into seven piles, the same way as before. Now, request the number of the pile containing the selected card. Mention that you have seen magicians ask their volunteers to repeat this part of the trick over and over, but you can see that your volunteer won't enjoy that, so twice will be enough.

5 Ask the volunteer to pile up the cards as before (second pile on the first, and third on the second, and so on). Then, ask her to start dealing them out one last time, one by one. After a while, stop her, and say the next card will be the card. And it will be!

6 How is this so? Well, the secret is simple mathematics. There is a formula to "predict" the correct card every time! Subtract 1 from the second pile number, and multiply the answer by 7. Add the first pile number to that answer, and the total is the position of the card in the deck.

7 So, if the card was in pile five the second time, and pile one the first time, the formula would be: 1 – 1 = 0; 0 x 7 = 0; 0 + 5 = 5. The fifth card dealt in the third round will be the chosen card. Often it will be a card in the 20s or 30s, that you'll be looking for.

5
CHAPTER

Trick 71

The amazing fruit prediction

★ **You need:** a table, an orange, a shoe box, wrapping paper, a hat, pieces of paper, a pen

This great trick relies on good talking skills and preparation. You'll make a prediction that a volunteer will correctly name a piece of fruit in a sealed box. Your audience will have lots of fun, as they all participate in this fruity trick!

1 Before the show, place an orange in a shoebox, or a box of similar size. Wrap the box in wrapping paper – try to use dark paper with stars and moons on it, for a magical effect.

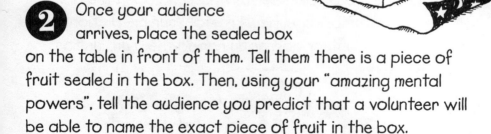

2 Once your audience arrives, place the sealed box on the table in front of them. Tell them there is a piece of fruit sealed in the box. Then, using your "amazing mental powers", tell the audience you predict that a volunteer will be able to name the exact piece of fruit in the box.

3 Now ask each member of the audience for the name of a fruit. They might say "apple".

Pretend to write the word on a piece of paper, fold it up, and drop it into your hat – but secretly write the word "orange", without the audience seeing.

4 Keep talking to the audience, as you take the names of different fruits. Keep writing the word "orange" on every piece of paper. You might pretend to have trouble spelling the name of a fruit, and toss the piece of paper away and write the word again. This will make it look as though you really are writing down all the fruit names. You need to use your good talking skills, to help fool the audience!

5 After everyone gives you the name of a fruit, ask a volunteer to choose a piece of paper from the hat. Of course, the word "orange" will be written on each piece.

6 Now have your volunteer unwrap and open the box, revealing the orange. Hey, Presto! Your prediction was correct - your volunteer correctly named the fruit, just as you said she would!

AAHRR... it's AN ORANGE!

5
CHAPTER

Trick 72
Banana Breaker!

★ **You need:** a banana, a long pin

Your audience will believe you really have magical powers when you perform this simple, but effective trick!

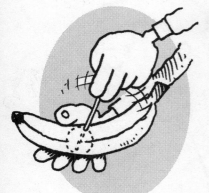

1 Prepare for this trick by carefully pushing the pin into the banana. Push the pin through the skin, but try not to make a big hole, and do not push it all the way through the skin on the other side of the banana. Wiggle the pin from side to side, so it cuts through the fruit inside the skin. Now pull the pin out.

2 Once your audience arrives, explain to them that you can use your mental powers to cut through objects. Tell them that to prove it you are going to cut a banana in half, without touching it.

3 Ask a volunteer to come up and help you. Warn them that they must hold the bottom of the banana and stand very still, so as not to get in the way of your razor-sharp mind!

4 Ask the audience for complete silence. Then place one finger on the side of your forehead, and look as though you are concentrating very hard. Suddenly, take your finger from your forehead, and point to the banana. Say, "Alakazam", and make a cutting motion with your finger.

5 Now tell your audience that the banana is cut in half. Have your volunteer peel the banana. When the skin is peeled, the banana will break in half where you cut it earlier with the pin. Amazing! Take a bow!

CHAPTER 5

Trick 73

Hocus pocus

★ **You need:** a set of dominoes, a calculator

This trick will show you why math is a magician's best friend! Remember, it's best not to have a formula while performing, so memorize the sequence before you do this trick.

1 Spread out the set of dominoes face down on the table, and ask a volunteer to choose one. He should not let you see which one he chose.

2 Give him the calculator, and ask him to do the following (as in the example below):

enter one of the domino's numbers	4
multiply that number by 5	= 20
add 7 to the total	= 27
double the new total	= 54
add the domino's other number to the result	= 56

3 Finally, ask your volunteer to hand the calculator to you with their answer still showing. Add a bit of hocus pocus to find out which domino they chose.

4 Slowly say the magic words "Ho-cus po-cus", push in "- 14 =" on the calculator, which in the example above would give you an answer of 42. Of course, 4 and 2 are the numbers on the chosen domino!

5 If your volunteer began his calculation by reversing the numbers (if he began the equation with 2 and added 4 later), the number on the calculator would be 24, as in 2 and 4. This is ok too!

IT WOULD BE A REALLY BIG HELP IF YOU COULD UNDO THE KNOT ... ... AHHRR ... NO ... IT'S NOT PART OF THE TRICK!

Riveting Rope and Ring Tricks

These tricks are lots of fun to perform. Ropes and rings are easy to get in all lengths and colors. Specialty magic shops sell linking rings, and every type of magic rope possible, so clever magicians can vary their tricks. Ropes and rings can also be found at some craft stores, or home improvement stores.

Trick 74
The absconding ring

★ **You need:** a rope, a ring, a handkerchief

This is a great trick to begin a routine. It looks like magic, so it must be magic!

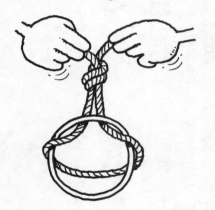

1 First, slip the rope through the ring, just as we've shown in the illustration. Make sure the ends of the rope are knotted together, so the ring is trapped.

2 Involve your audience by asking a volunteer to hold the knotted ends, while you hold the ring. Use the handkerchief to keep the ring out of sight.

3 Tell your audience you will need all your magical powers to free the ring without untying the rope! Tell the volunteer not to let go of the rope.

4 Tell a story, while you keep your hands out of sight behind the handkerchief. What you are doing with your hands is freeing the knot and pushing the rope downwards over the ring.

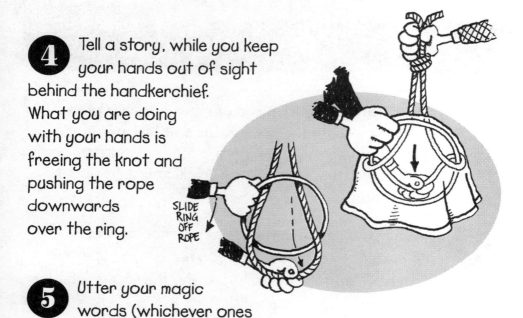

SLIDE RING OFF ROPE

5 Utter your magic words (whichever ones work best for you) as you free the ring, make sure the rope is still knotted and held by your volunteer. Here comes the wild applause!

A TRUE MAGICIAN!!

Trick 75
How long?

★ **You need:** a short piece of rope, a longer piece of rope—both the same color and texture

---

This is another easy-to-learn rope trick, great to do at the start of a show.

1 Prepare the ropes before the audience arrives. The audience needs to think you have two ropes of equal length knotted together. That's why the ropes must be the same color and thickness.

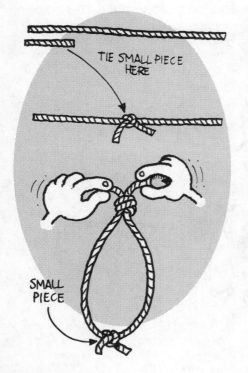

TIE SMALL PIECE HERE

SMALL PIECE

2 First, tie the short piece of rope around the centre of the long piece. Don't tie it too tightly. Tie the two ends of the long piece together as well. Does it look like you now have two pieces of rope of equal length tied together? If not, redo the knots, because that's the *most* important part of the trick.

3 Ready to perform?
Show the ropes to the
audience, holding them carefully in both hands. Tell them you
are able to make these two short pieces of rope into one
long piece because of your exceptional powers.

4 Untie the real knotted ends, and examine the rope
carefully. Make sure to mention the knot in the middle
of the rope. Say you're sure you'll be able to get rid of that
pesky knot by using a few magic words. In fact, it's a great

THE PESKY KNOT
(The SHORT ROPE)

idea to ask the people in
the audience for their
favorite magic words, and
use one or more of them.

5 While they are shouting out
their magic words, wind the
rope around your left hand. Don't
stop when you come to the false
knot, but actually hide it, in your right
hand, as you slide it along the longer rope.

SLIDE KNOT
ALONG THE
LONG ROPE

SIM
SALA
BIM!

6 Now is the best
time to mutter
more magic words, and
unwind the now
completely unknotted
rope from your left hand.
It's now one piece!

Trick 76

Scarf and rope separation

★ **You need:** A length of very thin rope or some string, a scarf, a table.

Amaze your audience with this trick, by separating a scarf and some rope that are tightly knotted together!

1 Before your show, make a small loop in the piece of rope, as shown.

2 Next, knot the scarf around the loop. Lay the scarf and rope out on the table, so the loop of rope is hidden underneath the knot in the scarf.

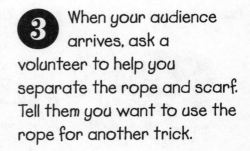

3 When your audience arrives, ask a volunteer to help you separate the rope and scarf. Tell them you want to use the rope for another trick.

4 Hold the scarf and rope in front of your volunteer. Pull tightly on the scarf, but do not pull on the rope.

152

Your audience will be fooled into thinking the scarf and rope are tightly knotted together!

5 Ask your volunteer to blow on the knot, to help separate the scarf and rope. Pull on the scarf again, but do not pull the rope. The two will not come undone.

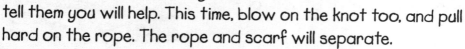

6 Ask your volunteer to blow on the knot again and tell them you will help. This time, blow on the knot too, and pull hard on the rope. The rope and scarf will separate.

To everyone's amazement, the scarf will remain knotted but you will be able to use the rope for your next trick!

Trick 77
Caught!

★ **You need:** a loop of string, a ring

In this trick, you'll catch a ring on a piece of string. You will need to perform a type of throw and flip which needs a lot of practice!

1 Make sure your audience sits in front of you for this trick.

2 Hold the loop of string downward in one hand, stretching it as wide as possible with your fingers spread. Put the ring beneath the loop of string. Then, bring the ring up, so the string is inside the ring. Position the ring about two-thirds of the way up the loop. Hold it with your four fingers above and your thumb below.

3 Now for the tricky part—the combination throw and flip you have perfected! You need to throw the ring hard down towards the bottom of the loop, and, at the same time, you need to flip the ring, so it turns and catches in a knot at the bottom of the loop.

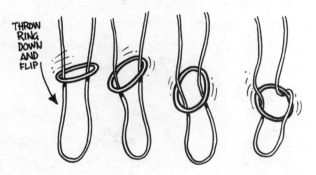

THROW RING DOWN AND FLIP

4 Once the ring is secured in the knot hold it up to wild applause from your audience.

5 By the way, be prepared to have the ring fall to the floor hundreds of times before you have perfected this trick! Don't give up—it looks wonderful in performance and your friends will love it!

Look old chap... I can make BIG BEN disappear!

I made the STATUE OF LIBERTY vanish for a full 5 minutes!

When did you see Mt Fuji last?

Did you know?
America, Germany, Japan and England have produced world famous magicians. Today, David Copperfield is the magician most people around the world have heard of. He has made a Lear jet disappear! His magic continues to astound.

Trick 78
The disappearing knot

★ **You need:** a piece of thick string (or cord) about 12 in. (30 cm) long, a matchbox cover

This is a terrific trick. Your audience will believe you can remove a knot from a piece of string!

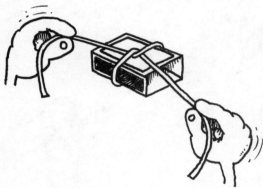

1 Using the illustration as a guide, take the string and tie a single knot around the matchbox cover, making sure one end leads off to the right.

2 Hold the matchbox cover upright, and poke one string end into the center of the box. Ask a volunteer to hold the end when it falls through the box.

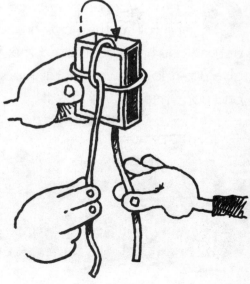

3 Gently—very gently—slide the whole knot off the cover and into the box. Make sure your volunteer is now holding both ends of the string.

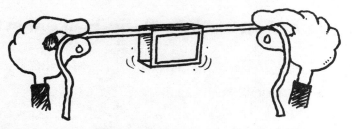

4 Here's where the magic comes in. Grasp the matchbox cover with your left hand, wave your other hand over it, and say several really great magic words, such as "Alikazam!"

5 With you still holding the matchbox cover, ask the volunteer to gently pull apart the ends of the string (which he is still holding of course). You can now slide the matchbox cover up and down the string showing the audience, and your volunteer the knot has completely gone!

NO
KNOT!

6 Hand the matchbox cover and string to any audience member who wishes to check your props!

Trick 79

Rope handcuffs

★ **You need:** two 24 in. (60 cm) lengths of cotton rope

You'll tie your audience up in knots with this trick! (Then you'll free them, of course!)

1 Ask for two brave volunteers. Tie their wrists together with the ropes as shown in the illustration.

2 Ask them to try really hard to release themselves from their predicament without cutting the rope or untying the knots. Of course, they won't be able to do so. You'll have to help them.

3 First, pull the middle of one of the ropes towards the opposite person, so you create a loop. Draw the loop to the wrist of that person, and pass the loop through the rope around the wrist. Pull it over the entire hand.

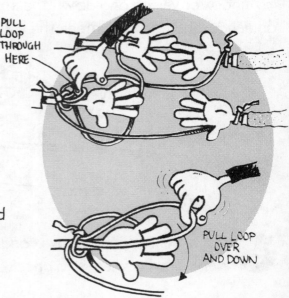

PULL LOOP THROUGH HERE

PULL LOOP OVER AND DOWN

4 Once this has occurred you have actually freed your volunteers from their rope handcuffs. Ask them to step back from each other. Now, take a bow!

Trick 80
Just one hand

★ **You need: one length of rope measuring 35 in. (90 cm)**

This is another great trick your audience will love to watch. Tie a knot in a rope using just one hand. The audience won't know how *you* did it!

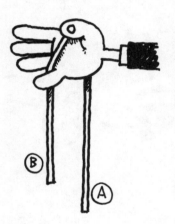

1 Make sure your audience sits in front of you. Drape the rope across your right hand, between the thumb and index finger, and behind the little finger. One end needs to be a little longer than the other (see illustration depicting A and B).

2 Give the rope an upward flick, and drop your hand down at the same time, so you catch the longer end of the rope (A) between your index and middle fingers.

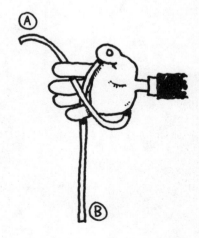

3 Now hold onto the A end of the rope and turn your hand so your fingers are facing the floor. The rest of the rope will slip off your hand, forming a one-handed knot!

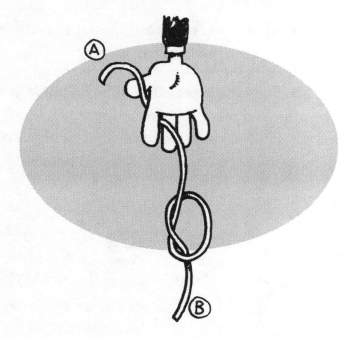

4 You will have to practice that upward flick—but it's worth it, as it's a classy trick when done with pizzazz!

Oooh...Aye ABRACADABRA! I think we might try a wee rabbit here. This haggis is not really doin' the trick!

Did you know?

Pulling a rabbit out of a hat is supposed to be a classic trick. However, it's a trick that is rarely performed. It was probably devised by Scottish magician John Henry Anderson in the 1830s.

Trick 81
Ring release

★ **You need:** **a piece of string 18 in. (45 cm) long, a large ring**

In this trick, you'll do the impossible and remove a large ring that's hanging from a piece of string. Think it sounds simple? Not if you can't slip the ring off either end of the string.

1 Once again, your audience needs to be seated in front of you for this trick.

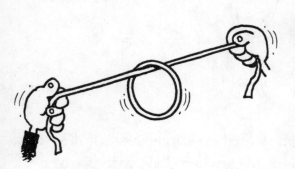

2 Slip the large ring on the string. Ask a volunteer to hold one end of the string, while you hold the other end. Make sure the string is taut and the ring is in the center of the string.

3 Hold the ring at the bottom, and turn it once towards you. Explain you are doing this to lock the ring on the string.

4 Now grasp the string where it joins the ring, and drop your end of the string. Put this end of the string through the ring.

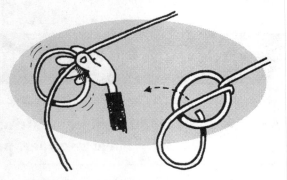

5 Again pull the string taut and tell your audience the ring is now "double locked" on to the string.

6 Grasp the ring and give it a spin. As it stops make sure the string in the center of the ring is on the bottom. If it isn't, simply turn it until it is.

7 Finally, grasp the ring and move it quickly back and forth on the string as you pull it towards you. The "locked" ring will come right off!

Trick 82

The prediction pendulum coin

★ **You need:** a piece of string, a coin with a hole,
a large sheet of paper, pencils, a table

You'll know, with the help of your trusty pendulum coin,
what your friends have written!

1 Before your show begins, thread the coin on
the string.

2 On with the show!
Tear the sheet of
paper into eight equal pieces,
and give the pieces to eight
people in your audience.
Ask four people to write
down the name of an animal,
and four people to write
down the name of a bird.

RRRIP!

3 One of the volunteers can then spread the pieces
of paper face-down on the table.

4 Hold the string with the coin above the pieces of
paper. Explain to your audience the coin will swing
over the pieces of paper with animals written on them,
but the coin will circle over the pieces of paper containing
bird names.

5 Make the coin swing or circle over each piece of paper, according to what you "see" there, and state whether it's an animal or bird. Immediately, turn over the piece of paper to show you're right!

I think I hear a cheep...cheep... under this one!

CHEEP-CHEEP

6 You have to be observant and remember two rules when doing this magic trick. First, when you tear the paper, don't use scissors! That's why we said tear it! The four corner pieces of the sheet of paper will have two smooth edges, and two rough edges. These go to the people you ask to write down an animal. The four middle pieces of paper will have three rough edges and one smooth. They go to the people writing bird names. When you do your pendulum predictions, you only have to remember to swing over the paper pieces with two smooth edges, indicating an animal, and circle over the paper pieces with one smooth edge.

Trick 83

The forever rope

★ **You need:** a piece of rope at least 35 in. (90 cm) long, a table, a wand, a jacket with an inside pocket

Your friends won't mind being strung along with this clever rope trick.

1 Show your audience you are holding a short piece of rope. (In fact, you are holding the ends of your long piece of rope, but more on that later.) Explain that your powers can make the rope grow.

2 Tap the back of one hand with your wand, and say some terrific magic words. Then begin to pull the rope from one end. It will continue to grow, and grow, and grow.

3 Continue to pull the rope, or even better, ask an audience member to do it. Once it is coiled on the table, take a bow as your audience applauds.

4 How is it done? It's simple really. Fold the rope in half, and make sure both ends are held in your hand. Thread the rest of the rope up your jacket sleeve and into the inside pocket.

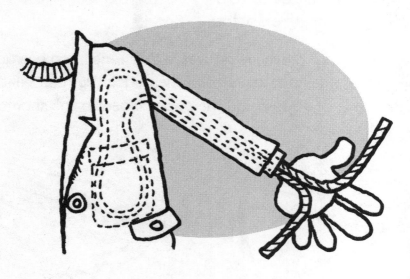

Trick 84

Cut and restored rope

★ **You need:** A pair of scissors, a square piece of paper, a piece of thin rope or thick string.

This is a classic trick all magicians need to perfect. You will be able to cut a piece of rope in half, then restore it. Practice hard before your show, until you can do the trick smoothly.

1 Before your show, prepare the piece of paper. Carefully make two folds in it, so it has a bottom and two sides. One of the sides should be a little taller than the other, but should not fold completely across the bottom.

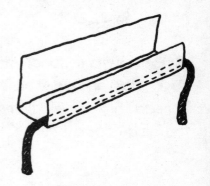

2 Once your audience arrives, explain that you are going to cut the rope in half, and then magically restore it. Lay the piece of rope inside the paper, close to the shorter side of the paper.

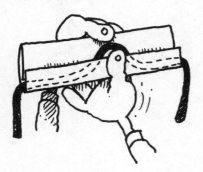

3 Now for the tricky part! Fold the paper over the rope. Be sure to fold the tallest side down first. When you fold the shorter side down, catch the rope with your thumb and slightly pull it out of the paper. (See illustration 2 & 3) Tip the paper so the folds are facing away from your audience. Then they will not see what you are doing.

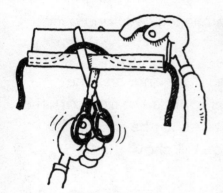

4 Hold the paper and rope up to the audience, and use your scissors to cut through the paper. Be sure to cut underneath the piece of rope you pulled out with your thumb. Cut all the way through the paper. Your audience will think you've cut the rope, too!

5 Crumple the paper and rope in your hand. Say the magic words "Abracadabra." Then slowly pull the rope away from the paper. Voila, the cut rope is restored!

6 Show your audience the two pieces of paper. They won't be able to figure out how you "restored" the rope!

Trick 85

Two rings and a rope

★ **You need:** two rings, a piece of rope

You cannot get this trick wrong! It's quick and easy to perform. You can dazzle the same audience over and over with *your* magical skills.

1 First, thread the rope through both rings. Tell the audience there are two ways to take the rings off the rope. One, of course, is to slide the rings to the end of the rope. The other is the magic way! You will show them.

2 Use your left thumb and index finger to hold the rope, and one ring firmly at the point marked A on the illustration. Hold the other ring with your right thumb at point B.

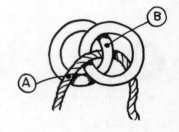

3 Quickly pull your right hand back toward your body, and off the end of the rope. This movement will take the ring which was held in your right hand off the rope. At the same time, you will see the ring held in your left hand miraculously pass through the rope as well!

4 Just wait for the applause! You can do this trick several times for the same audience. They won't be able to see anything but magic!

Fun with Magic

This is what we hope all your magic tricks will lead to—lots of fun. There is no real theme to the following tricks, as there has been with the ring, rope, and coin tricks. In fact, the only thing they have in common is—yes, you've guessed it—they're fun!

Trick 86
You can do what?

> ★ **You need:** 10 magazines (or books) with at least 27 pages, a calculator, and a table.

Yes, you can read minds. You'll prove it with this easy trick.

1 To prepare for this trick, place the magazines in a pile on the table, and study page 27 in the fourth magazine from the top. Check that page for key words or pictures – anything that is outstanding.

2 Give an audience member the calculator, and ask her to do the following:

Enter any number between 1 and 100 (for example, 46).

Add 28	= 74
Multiply by 6	= 444
Subtract 3	= 441
Divide by 3	= 147

Subtract 3 more than the
original number (46 + 3 = 49)   = 98

Add 8   = 106

Subtract 1 less than the
original number (46 − 1 = 45)   = 61

Multiply by 7   = 427

The answer will always be 427!

3 Turn your back to the audience, and ask your
volunteer to look at the first digit of her calculation.
She must not tell you what it is; instead she should count out
that number of magazines from the top of the pile.

4 Ask her to look at
the final two digits (27)
and turn to that page in
the magazine. She should
hold that page up to
show the audience.

My favorite page in the magazine too!

5 Ask everyone, to
concentrate on what
they can see on the page, so you
can read their minds. Of course, you'll have no problems; you
have already studied this page! Dazzle your audience by
announcing what is on the page!

Trick 87

Faster than a calculator

★ **You need:** a pen or pencil, a piece of paper, a calculator

---

Amaze your friends (and your parents!) by adding up five three-digit numbers in a few seconds, without using a calculator!

1 There is no need to prepare anything for this. You'll just need your math skills!

2 Ask a volunteer to write down a three-digit number on the piece of paper. The digits must be different, and cannot form a pattern, such as 1, 2, 3.

3 Ask your volunteer to repeat step 2. The three-digit numbers must be different.

4 Ask for one more three-digit number to be written down underneath the first two. This number is the one you are really concerned with—it is the key number.

5 Now take the pen and paper, and write a fourth number. Make sure the sum of the first and fourth numbers equals 999.

613
184
205
386
815

6 Write another number, making sure the sum of the second and fifth numbers equals 999.

7 Give the paper back to your volunteer and ask him to use the calculator to add the five numbers—you are not to see the total.

8 When he returns the paper to you (the total is not written on it), pretend to add up the five numbers in your head within seconds. Write down the total. It will match what he has on the calculator.

9 How? Well, remember we said the third number is the key number? It's part of a simple formula, which is:

$$2000 + (\text{key number} - 2) = \text{the answer}$$

An example:

Volunteer's first number	613
Volunteer's second number	184
Volunteer's third and key number	205
Your number to make 999	386
Your number to make 999	+ 815
	= 2203

$$2000 + (205 - 2) = 2203$$

10 If your volunteer writes a 9 for the first digit anywhere, add it up to 999, but write down a two-digit number; don't bother with the 0 in front.

Trick 88

In a tearing hurry

★ **You need:** two pieces of paper

This is a quick trick you can only do once for an audience. It's a great show-opener, or can be a bit of light relief after a long trick.

1 Before your audience arrives, make two tears in each of the two pieces of paper, creating three equal strips on each sheet. Do not tear through the sheets completely.

2 Once your audience is seated, ask for a volunteer. Hand your volunteer one of the pieces of paper. Ask her to tear the two end pieces from the middle piece in just one tear. She won't be able to do it, but you can!

3 Pick up the other piece of paper and show her how it's done. Hold one end piece in each hand. Bend over, and hold the middle piece with your lips. Pull the outside pieces, and you will be left with three separate pieces of paper!

Trick 89

The amazing jumping rubber band

★ **You need:** several colored rubber bands

You only have to learn one secret move in order to perform this simple sleight-of-hand trick, but your audience will think you're an amazing magician!

1 Let the audience see you put a rubber band around two fingers, then you should close your hand.

2 As you close your hand, secretly stretch the rubber band and slip all four fingertips inside it. You must do this quickly and secretly. You will need to practice getting all four fingertips into the rubber band with a minimum of movement. Just make it look as if you are making sure your fingers are comfortable. When you look at your hand, you can see the rubber band stretched over the four fingers, but the audience cannot.

3 Open and close your hand. The band automatically (and magically!) jumps to the other two fingers.

4 Of course, now you want to make it jump back again. Put all four fingers into the band as you close your hand; then open and close your hand. See! The band jumps again. It works every time, once you get the hang of it!

5 If your audience is sitting, or standing close to you, and you want to vary the trick, use two different colored rubber bands and put all four fingertips into both. When you open and close your hand, the bands will magically swap places.

Trick 90

The messy trick

★ **You need: three eggs, three cardboard toilet rolls, one broom, a plate, three glasses half-full of water**

In this trick, you're going to make three eggs drop into glasses of water! You'll probably make a mess while you are learning this one—so don't forget to clean up the kitchen when you've finished practicing!

1 Choose your location—an outside picnic table is a good place to do this trick.

2 Allow your audience to stand around, but not too close to the table.

3 Set up the trick on the edge of the table. The eggs should sit on top of the cardboard rolls. Make sure the eggs are the right size. If they are too small or too large to sit properly on the rolls, the trick won't work. The cardboard rolls should sit on the plate, and the plate should sit on top of the glasses (see illustration). Check that the plate is hanging over the edge of the table.

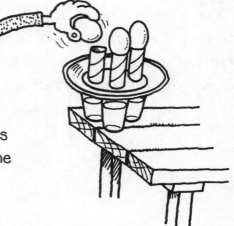

CHAPTER 7

4 Face the table and place the broom in front of you. The bristles of the broom must be below the pie plate. Step on the bristles while pulling the handle of the broom back towards you.

5 As you let go, the handle of the broom will hit the pie plate straight on and things will fly!

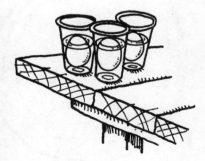

6 The three eggs will fall into the half-full glasses of water! Clever magician!

Trick 91
Stay awake!

★ **You need:** three or four dark-colored balloons, an equal number of light-colored balloons, string, a pin, a wand

---

You'll keep audiences awake, when you show them how you change the color of a balloon!

1 This trick requires preparation. First, insert your light-colored balloons inside the darker ones. Now inflate each inner (light) balloon, then tie its neck with some string.

2 Now inflate each outer balloon to create an air space between each balloon. Tie the necks of the outer balloons. Secure the same piece of string to the neck of the outer balloon.

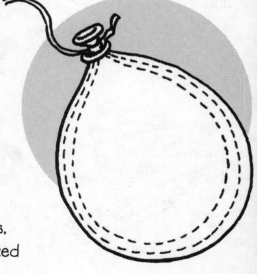

3 Attach a pin to the end of your wand. You want to make a bang! Prick one of the outer balloons, and your audience will be amazed to see it change color.

(If you burst both balloons at once, just tell the members of your audience you thought they looked sleepy and they'll miss the next wonderful trick if they doze off!)

4 Hang the balloons around the stage area so you can easily reach them during a performance. Make sure your audience notices the balloons by referring to them: "I'm surrounded by some fabulous purple balloons, but I do prefer yellow."

5 If you feel the audience is not appreciative enough during any part of your show—touch one of the (outer) balloons with your wand and bang! Not only do people wake up, they realize you've changed the color of the balloon! Burst the balloons throughout your act, ensuring no one sleeps!

Trick 92
Fruit or vegetable?

> ★ **You need:** a sheet of paper, three pencils, a hat

Sometimes the simplest tricks are the best. Well, this is one of the best!

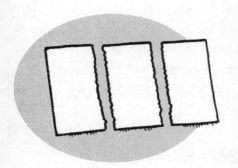

1 Prepare for the trick before your audience arrives by tearing a sheet of paper into three equal portions. The trick here is in the tearing. You need to be able to feel the uneven edges of the pieces of paper to enable you to complete the trick. So don't use scissors!

2 Once the audience arrives, ask for three volunteers to come forward to help you with the trick. Hand two volunteers pieces of paper with only one torn edge, that is a piece taken from the end of the original sheet. Ask them to write the name of any fruit on the paper. They are not to show you.

3 At the same time, hand one volunteer the other piece of paper which has two torn sides. Ask him to write down the name of a vegetable.

HMMM.... A VEGETABLE

2 TORN SIDES

Try to be casual about which piece of paper you give to each volunteer, but make sure they get the "right" ones!

MIX
MIX
MIX

4 If you have enough members in the audience, ask a fourth volunteer to come forward and place the three pieces of paper into the hat and mix them up.

5 Tell the audience you are able to pull out only the paper with the vegetable named on it. Reach into the hat, making a big deal out of the fact you can't see the pieces of paper. Feel quickly for the piece of paper with two torn sides. *Voilá!* There is your vegetable!

Apple

CARROT

Banana

Trick 93
Free-standing pencil

★ **You need:** a pencil with an eraser end, a display pin

Everything you touch is affected by your magic. You'll prove it by making a pencil stand on its own. Or at least that's what your audience will see, as long as you hide the pin at the end of the trick and don't let audience members get too close!

1 Before the show begins, push the pin into the eraser.

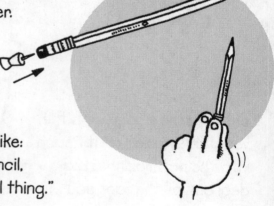

2 Stand in front of your audience and hold up the pencil by the eraser. Hide the pin with your fingers. Say something like: "See, it's just an ordinary pencil, but in my hands it's a magical thing."

3 Bring up your other hand with its palm facing up and, at the same time, turn your body so the side with the hand holding the pencil is facing the audience.

While you are turning and your fingers are still hiding the pin from view, place the eraser end of the pencil at the base of the middle and ring fingers of your other hand. The pin slides between these fingers and is held in place by your fingers.

4 Here comes the magic! Slowly remove the hand that was originally holding the pencil, preferably while uttering some magic chant. Keep your other hand completely still. It will look as if the pencil is magically standing upright in the palm of your hand.

5 After everyone has had their fill of watching the pencil stand for a few moments, remove it with a flourish and a bow! Keep the pin hidden in your fingers.

6 Offer people in the audience a look at the pencil to assure themselves it is just an ordinary pencil.

Trick 94
Soft penetrates hard

★ **You need:** a raw potato with its skin on,
some drinking straws

Most people wouldn't believe a flimsy drinking straw could
pierce a hard, raw potato, but you know better. Right?

1 Lead into this trick by
giving an audience member the
potato and a straw. Challenge her to
push the straw into the potato. She
will fail, so provide her with some
more straws. They'll just
break, and the potato will
remain undamaged.

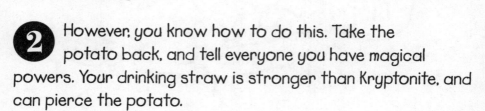

2 However, you know how to do this. Take the
potato back, and tell everyone you have magical
powers. Your drinking straw is stronger than Kryptonite, and
can pierce the potato.

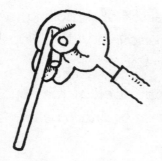

3 Fold over the top of
the straw, and grip it
tightly in your fist (see
illustration), with the rest of
the straw sticking out.

4 Grip the potato in the palm of your other hand.

5 Chant magical words and "embrace" your magical powers. Then bring down the straw very quickly, stabbing the potato. Because of the closed top of the straw, the air within is compressed. This makes the straw rigid. Practice until the straw goes through the peel and into the potato.

Trick 95
What a corker!

★ **You need:** two equally sized corks

You'll become a master illusionist with this trick, but be prepared for many hours of practice! You need to perfect the movements that will convince the audience they are seeing two corks pass through each other!

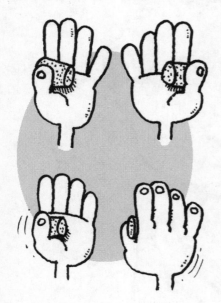

1 Hold one cork in each hand between your thumb and index finger. Have both palms vertical, so they are facing you.

2 Keep the corks in place, but rotate your dominant hand so it is palm away from you. (If you are right-handed, this will be your right hand, if you are left-handed, it will be your left hand.)

3 Grip the other hand's cork with your dominant hand by placing your index finger on top of the cork and the thumb on the bottom.

4 At the same time, grip the cork in your dominant hand with the other hand the same way you did last time. To do this, reach the thumb under the fingers of your dominant hand to grip one end of the cork, while your index finger grips the other end. This sounds a lot more complicated that it really is.

5 Now separate your hands, taking away the opposite corks. As your hands move apart, rotate them again. The hand which was palm out before is now palm in and the hand which was palm in is now palm out.

6 The secret is to practice the movements. When it's done smoothly, it creates the illusion of the two corks passing through each other. Watch it in a mirror while you practice. You'll know when you're ready for an audience.

Trick 96
Coin of illusion

★ **You need:** a pocketful of change

Although you need many coins for this trick—you use none!
Your audience will think you are throwing a coin from hand
to hand, but it's all an illusion!

1 Make a show of taking a handful of coins from your
pocket. Let the audience see the coins are real.
Choose one coin and pretend to pick it up. You'll need to
practice this! Return the coins to your pocket.

ONLY PRETEND THERE'S A COIN

SNAP FINGERS ONTO HERE FOR A SNAP SOUND
(LIKE A COIN HITTING!)

SNAP

2 Throw the imaginary
coin back and forth
from one hand to the other.
Make a small slapping sound
as you pretend to catch the
coin each time. Practice with
a real coin so you can get the
sound right. If you loosen
your fingers and slap the heel
of your palm as you "catch"
your coin, it should sound OK.

3 Do this several times, then stop and pretend to hold the imaginary coin in one hand. Ask you audience to guess how it landed, "Heads or tails?" Of course, upon opening your hand there is no coin. That's OK because the audience assumes it's now in your other hand.

4 Slowly open your other hand to reveal no coin there either. Take a bow while your audience applauds!

You should know enough about MAGIC now to know just how I do this trick...!
1... 2 ....3 ...

BANG

Trick 97
How many pieces?

> ★ **You need: two strips of paper about 20 in. (50 cm) by 4 in. (10 cm), a black marker pen, glue**

This is a classic destroy and restore trick!

1 Before your audience arrives, write the words ONE PIECE on each of the two strips of paper. Make the letters look exactly the same on both strips.

2 Fold one strip in half, then in half again, and again, until the paper measures about 2 in. (5 cm) long and 3 in. (7.5 cm) wide.

3 Glue this tightly folded square to the back of the other strip of paper. Glue it near the end of the strip behind the word ONE.

4 Now, you are ready for an audience. Hold your strip of paper by the ends, so your audience sees the words ONE PIECE. Tell your audience you have just the one piece of paper.

5 Now tear the strip of paper in half. You must be careful not to expose the paper glued on the back. Place the torn off strip in front of the piece with *ONE* on it, and hold them at the ends.

8 SMALL PIECES

6 Say you'd like it smaller, so tear both pieces of paper in half again, putting the pieces on your left side in front of the others again. Tear them one last time. You should now have eight pieces.

7 Fold the pieces, keeping the edges away from you, and even with the secret folded piece of paper. Are you holding a packet of folded paper between your fingers and thumb of your right hand? You should be. The audience only sees torn pieces of paper, but you can see one whole strip.

8 Look confused, and say something like: "But now I've done this, I really think I prefer it as one piece." As you say this, pass the folded packet over to your left hand, and turn it around. The strip which is still in one piece should now be facing the audience.

9 Once your fingers and thumb have secured the packet, wave your hand over it and chant a few magic words. Now, dramatically open the strip, so the audience can see the words ONE PIECE, apparently whole again!

HOLD TORN PIECES BEHIND HERE

ONE PIECE

10 The torn pieces are folded together so they shouldn't separate and fall to the floor. If they do, keep practicing!

Trick 98
Any color

★ **You need: three different colored crayons, a table**

You can choose the correct colored crayon every time—without looking!

1 Prepare for this trick by marking each of the crayons in a different way. You need to be able to tell which crayon is which by just feeling them. The marks, of course, cannot be obvious to anyone looking at the crayons. So, for instance, you might tear a piece of the paper from one, make a nick in the bottom of another with your fingernail, and make a nick in the top of the third one. Only you know which mark matches which color, and, naturally, you must remember this!

2 With this trick, it's important to be dramatic! You don't want your audience to notice that you are feeling for the mark on a particular crayon, so you need to distract them. Tell your audience that you're concentrating hard, trying to "sense" the colors.

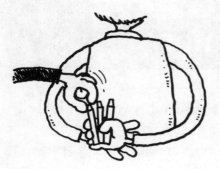

3 To perform the trick, ask a volunteer to randomly place the crayons into your hands, which you are holding behind your back.

RED

4 Now, face your audience, and ask the volunteer to call out one of the colors. Start acting, while you feel for the mark of the particular color called.

5 When you find the crayon, bring it out with a flourish and wait for the applause. Only do this trick once in a show.

THAT LOOKS LIKE RED TO ME...! DO I HAVE EYES IN THE BACK OF MY HEAD..?

Trick 99
Hidey ho

> ★ **You need:** a deck of cards, a large scarf
> (or handkerchief)

You're such a good magician that any card you name can penetrate a solid object, such as a scarf!

1 All you have to do beforehand is secretly memorize the top card in the deck. Then, remember not to shuffle the cards!

MEMORIZED CARD NOW ON BOTTOM OF DECK

2 Hold the deck face-up in the palm of your left hand, if you're right-handed; or in your right, if you are left-handed. The card you have memorized should be sitting on the bottom of the deck in your palm.

3 Show the scarf to the audience. In fact, pass it around so everyone can see it's an ordinary scarf.

4 Once it's returned to you, drape the scarf over the deck of cards so its center rests on top of the deck.

5 Make sure you tell the audience you can't see the cards because the scarf is covering the deck. Reach under the scarf with your other hand, and remove the deck, but leave the memorized card under the scarf in your palm.

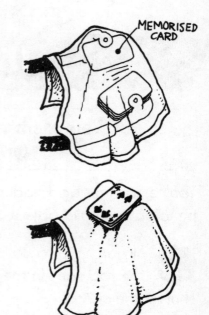

MEMORISED CARD

6 Place the deck of cards on top of the scarf, directly over the card that is hidden under the scarf.

7 Begin to wrap the deck of cards in the scarf. Start by folding the edge nearest you away from you with your free hand. Place the thumb of this hand underneath the card in your opposite palm and the wrapped deck. Place the rest of the fingers of that hand on top to grip the deck, and now revolve it upright so the hidden card faces you. Do this part carefully, because if you allow the hidden card to shift the audience will see it!

8 Now, keep the hand gripping the package where it is, use your opposite hand to fold the sides of the scarf back toward you, diagonally over the hidden card. The folds need to overlap this card, while your thumb holds everything in place.

9 It's time to dazzle your audience! With the fist of the hand that folded the scarf, grip all of the scarf hanging below and rotate the deck (keeping the hidden card facing you), so it is hanging down. If the folds are tight enough, the hidden card should stay in place when you lift your thumb.

10 Tell your audience that you can magically make any card you call appear through the scarf. Now, of course, you call the card you have memorized—the hidden card. Then shake the deck, while chanting magic words. The hidden card will magically begin to appear as if it is penetrating the center of the scarf. When it hits the table, allow the wrapped deck to be examined as you are basking in your audience's admiration!

SHAKE

SHAKE

Trick 100
Counting cards

★ **You need:** a deck of cards

This is a simple "find the card" trick that works on its own, but you can make it yours with some cleverly planned story.

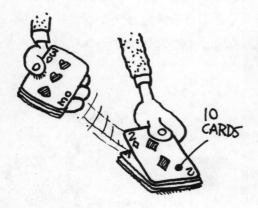

10 CARDS

1 Count out the top 10 cards from a deck of cards, but don't let your audience guess that you are counting. Use a story to distract the audience while you set up the trick.

2 When you've counted out 10 cards, sweep them up, and return them to the top of the deck. Secretly glance at the bottom card. Let's say it's the eight of clubs.

MEMORIZE THIS CARD!

7
CHAPTER

3 Ask the audience, or a particular person in the audience, for a number between 10 and 20. If the number chosen is 20, the trick won't work, so you need to have the audience choose a number between 10 and 20. If the number you're given is 14, count out 14 cards.

14 CARDS

4 Put the rest of the deck to one side, and add the digits of the chosen number, 1 and 4, together. You get 5.

5 Deal out five cards from the packet, and the fifth card will be the eight of spades!

SMALL PILE

CARD Nº 5 will be 8 of SPADES

Trick 101

A no-card card trick

> ★ **You need:** a pack of cards, your mind,
> and a good story

Finally, here's a card trick you can perform when you don't have a pack of cards handy.

1 Ask an audience member to choose a number between one and ten. Then tell him to change his mind, and choose another number! He shouldn't tell anyone the second number, but ask him to double it.

2 Now, ask him to add 14 to it. Then divide by 2, and subtract the original number. The answer is the value of his imaginary card. He must remember it.

3 For example:

First choice	3
Second number	4
Double it	8
Add 14	22
Divide by 2	11
Subtract original (−4)	7

7

CHAPTER

4 Now ask him to concentrate on a suit of cards—either hearts, clubs, diamonds, or spades. Pretend to concentrate, and then blurt out a suit, for instance, "Diamonds."

5 It is unlikely your first guess will be right, so keep guessing until you name the right suit.

6 Of course, the audience now thinks you're having trouble with the trick, as you probably took a few guesses to get the right suit. But, as soon as you guess the suit, you say something like: "Boy, I can't believe you chose the seven of hearts (or whatever)."

7 Pause here, you need your volunteer to realize you chose the correct value of the card.

8 This is really a simple trick. If you ask your volunteer to add 14, the final number will be 7; if you ask him to add 10, the final number will be 5, and so on. The answer is always going to be half of the number you ask him to add.

You're the greatest magician I know!

A

B

C

☆ ☆ ☆ ☆ ☆